Community Matters

Institute for Philosophy and Public Policy Studies
General Editor: Verna V. Gehring

About the Series. This new series grows out of a collaboration between the Institute for Philosophy and Public Policy at the University of Maryland and Rowman & Littlefield Publishers. Each slim volume in the series offers an insightful, accessible collection of essays on a current topic of real public concern, and which lies at the intersection of philosophy and public policy. As such, these books are ideal resources for students and lay readers, while at the same time making a distinctive contribution to the broader scholarly discourse.

About the Institute. Established in 1976 at the University of Maryland and now part of the School of Public Affairs, the Institute for Philosophy and Public Policy was founded to conduct research into the conceptual and normative questions underlying public policy formation. This research is conducted cooperatively by philosophers, policy makers and analysts, and other experts both within and outside of government. The Institute publishes the journal *Philosophy & Public Policy Quarterly* and the series Institute for Philosophy and Public Policy Studies with Rowman & Littlefield Publishers.

War after September 11

Genetic Prospects: Essays on Biotechnology, Ethics, and Public Policy

The Internet in Public Life

Community Matters: Challenges to Civic Engagement in the 21st Century

Community Matters

Challenges to Civic Engagement in the 21st Century

EDITED BY VERNA V. GEHRING

ROWMAN & LITTLEFIELD PUBLISHERS, INC.
Lanham • Boulder • New York • Toronto • Oxford

ROWMAN & LITTLEFIELD PUBLISHERS, INC.

Published in the United States of America
by Rowman & Littlefield Publishers, Inc.
A wholly owned subsidiary of The Rowman & Littlefield Publishing Group, Inc.
4501 Forbes Boulevard, Suite 200, Lanham, Maryland 20706
www.rowmanlittlefield.com

PO Box 317
Oxford
OX2 9RU, UK

British Library Cataloguing in Publication Information Available

Library of Congress Cataloging-in-Publication Data

Community matters : challenges to civic engagement in the 21st century / edited by
Verna V. Gehring.
    p. cm. -- (Institute for Philosophy and Public Policy studies)
    Includes index.
    ISBN 0-7425-4959-3 (hardcover : alk. paper) -- ISBN 0-7425-4960-7 (pbk. : alk. paper)
    1. Political participation. I. Gehring, Verna V. II. Series.

    JF799.C66 2005
    323'.042'0973--dc22   2005012657

Printed in the United States of America

♾™ The paper used in this publication meets the minimum requirements of American
National Standard for Information Sciences—Permanence of Paper for Printed Library
Materials, ANSI/NISO Z39.48-1992.

Contents

Contents

III: Service in Deed?: Civic Engagement and the Prospect of Mandatory Military Service

Preface

Several of the essays in this work first appeared as articles in *Philosophy & Public Policy Quarterly*, the journal sponsored by the Institute for Philosophy and Public Policy at the School of Public Policy, University of Maryland. William A. Galston, director of the Institute for Philosophy and Public Policy, contributed the introduction, as well as two chapters, and research scholars Peter Levine and Robert K. Fullinwider also contributed one chapter each. This volume has benefited from the conversation and thought of all of the research scholars at the Institute for Philosophy and Public Policy: William A. Galston, David A. Crocker, Robert K. Fullinwider, Peter Levine, Xiaorong Li, Judith Lichtenberg, Mark Sagoff, Jerome M. Segal, Robert Wachbroit, and David Wasserman, and the editor is grateful for all of their helpful comments and thoughtful advice in the development of this volume. Many thanks also go to Carroll Linkins and Richard Chapman for their help and kindness in bringing the essays to press.

Verna V. Gehring
Editor
Institute for Philosophy and Public Policy
School of Public Policy, University of Maryland
College Park, Maryland

The Challenge of Civic Engagement: An Introduction

William A. Galston

The idea of the "civic" is one of the most resonant in the history of the West. As many know, it descends directly from the Latin terms for city and citizenship, and English dictionaries typically define it as that which pertains to political communities, citizens, or citizenship. The idea of the civic denotes not only empirical realities or legal relations, but also a certain moral orientation. Persons are said to be "civic minded" when they care about their community as a whole, not just about themselves, and when they are prepared to act in accordance with that wider sphere of concern, even at some cost to themselves.

Perennial Challenges of Civic Life

The *making* of a citizen. This volume, the fourth in the series of Institute for Philosophy and Public Policy Studies, addresses three perennial challenges of civic life. In the first place, citizens are made, not born. Since at least the time of the ancient Greeks, philosophers, statesmen, and educators have debated both the contents of civic education and the arenas in which it should be conducted. From the beginning, families (including extended families) and military training were proposed as key sites. Aristotle was among the first to lament the absence of public education, a theme John Stuart Mill reiterated as recently as the mid-nineteenth century. Because mandatory

1

public education is now universal in advanced societies, formal schooling has emerged as a potentially important element of civic education. Evidence suggests that at least in the United States, schools have not come close to fulfilling their civic mission, either for well-to-do students or for lower-income and minority groups. The articles in Part I discuss why this under-performance is a matter of concern and suggest strategies for improvement.

How citizens are to agree (and disagree). Civic matters affect all members of a community and are thus of potential concern to all. This feature of civic life becomes especially important when, as is often the case, a community is divided in its views but is nonetheless called upon to choose a single course of action that binds all its members. A state's flag can either include or exclude symbols of the Confederacy, but not both. Public funds can either be supplied or denied to institutions espousing controversial views. Civic life, especially when grappling with symbolic issues, is thus bound to generate intense controversy. This kind of controversy is the focus of the essays in Part II.

Every community faces the challenge of containing controversy so as to avoid violence and maintain essential unity. One approach is to remove as many contested matters as possible from public determination by allowing individuals and groups to go their own way. As we have already seen, however, this is not always possible. And even when it is, the outcome may still be controversial. (Imagine a policy that attempts to eliminate controversies about public schooling by handing out educational vouchers to every family.) Another approach is to delegate decision making on a range of controversial issues either to experts or to institutions insulated from public pressure. As the reaction to the decision of the Massachusetts Supreme Court mandating gay marriage illustrates, the strategy of delegation is far from a reliable formula for avoiding civic strife. A third strategy is to acknowledge that it almost never possible to exclude the public, however divided, from weighing in on controversial issues. The task then becomes creating processes structured to increase the ratio of light to heat in public discussion. The burgeoning interest, practical as well as theoretical, in mechanisms of public "deliberation" embodies just this hope.

Citizens and service. A third perennial civic issue is how to define the rights and the responsibilities of citizenship. From Greek and Roman times down to the present, the allocation of the burden of national defense has been at the heart of citizenship, so understood. At their nation's inception, Americans mistrusted standing armies and sought to rely on local militias that would spring into action when necessary. For much of the twentieth century, however, the United States relied on a national draft to provide much of the military power needed to discharge expanding global obligations. The Vietnam debacle catalyzed a decision to abolish the draft and to rely on volunteers to meet military requirements.

While that is where matters stand today, more than three decades after the inception of the All-Volunteer Armed Forces, mounting doubts may spark a reconsideration. Few doubt that the current system has yielded a highly trained and effective fighting force. But the burden imposed by the occupation and economic/social/political reconstruction of Iraq has diminished the appeal of military service, raising the possibility that suitable volunteers may no longer come forward in sufficient numbers. For some, moreover, the quantity and quality of volunteers is not the sole point. They argue that civic life is diminished when only a small percentage of citizens shoulder the sacrifices of national defense and when the majority of elected officials have no direct knowledge of the matters of war and peace they are charged with deciding. Part III of this volume lays out key arguments on several sides of this issue.

The topics taken up in this slim volume are only a small subset of the rich conversation about civic life in the United States and around the world. It is our hope that these essays will encourage students, academics, and interested citizens outside the academy to go farther and dig deeper into these vital issues.

The Challenge of Civic Education

I

Solving the Civic Achievement Gap in *De Facto* Segregated Schools

Meira Levinson

"So why did the Articles of Confederation make it so hard for the states to work together and get anything done? Adam, what do you think?"

"Ummm—oh, Dr. Levinson, there's someone knocking at the door. Can I let them in?"

"No, I'll get it!"

"No, me, no, me!"

"I'm the closest!"

Josephine triumphantly makes it to the door first, and opens it to reveal my colleague Ms. Donis, who is visibly shaken. "Dr. Levinson, have you heard?"

"No, heard what?"

"The World Trade Center has been hit by two planes. There are rumors that the Pentagon has also been bombed, and maybe the Capitol Building. Do you have a TV in your classroom? No? Why don't you bring your students into my room; you all can watch the news with us."

Stunned, I line up my homeroom, nineteen eighth-grade students whom I first met only a week ago, and file them down the hall to Ms. Donis's room. We enter silently, filling in the extra desks and perching on the radiators in the back of her classroom. A thirteen-inch TV is propped on a chair in the front showing a wavy, often static-obscured image of Tom Brokaw and the World Trade Center towers pouring smoke and flames from gashes in their sides.

We watch for about forty-five minutes, long enough to see the first tower collapse, to learn that the Pentagon was indeed hit, and to hear more rumors about other missing, pos-

7

sibly hijacked planes. Although I am loathe to leave, my students are starting to get rest-less and the news is admittedly repetitive. Also, we're due in the library in half an hour to check out textbooks for the year, and I want to have an opportunity first to discuss with them what we have seen. Quietly, I motion to my homeroom students to follow me back to our classroom.

After my students slip into their seats, I ask them if they have any questions or thoughts. I'm surprised to find myself hit with a barrage.

"I don't understand what's happening. Can you explain it, Dr. Levinson?"

"Are the World Trade Center towers in Manhattan or Washington?"

"Where's the Pentagon?"

"I couldn't see anything. Why were those buildings collapsing?"

I realize that I'm going to have to explain everything that we just saw on television. Whether it's because of the fuzzy picture or the difficulty my thirteen and fourteen year-old charges have interpreting the raw, undigested nature of breaking news, many of my students are totally confused about what's going on. I pull a student desk to the front of the classroom and sit on its top, resting my feet on the seat of the attached chair. "Well," I begin, "I don't know more than you do, but it seems that some planes were hijacked and flown into buildings. Two were flown into the two towers of the World Trade Center, which is in Manhattan, and one was flown into the Pentagon, which is in Washington. We don't know yet if there are other places that have been attacked, and it seems that there are still some planes missing, which may also have been hijacked."

"Why would somebody attack the Pentagon?" DaQuin interrupts.

"Because it's the center of the American military. It's the symbol of America's military power," I answer.

"Oh." I discover that many of my students have never heard of the Pentagon, and most are confused about why it's named after a shape they learn about in math class. I go to the board and draw the building for them and explain its purpose; understanding starts to dawn.

"I saw the World Trade Center when I was in Manhattan last year," Anna volunteers.

"Yes, you can see it from many places in New York City," I answer.

"Wait," Yasmine asks. "Are Manhattan and New York City the same?"

I realize that I have to back up some more. As I will learn over the next few months, less than half of my students are native-born citizens. Although most have lived in the United States for many years, some since birth, few have traveled outside of Massachusetts within the continental United States; if they travel in the summer or over school holidays, it's to go "home" to Cape Verde, Puerto Rico, the Dominican Republic, Haiti, Jamaica, or Vietnam. Except for the few students who have visited relatives in New York, none has heard of the World Trade Center before today, so I draw a crude map of southern Manhattan on the board, filling in the twin towers, the Stock Exchange, Wall Street, showing why the area symbolizes America's economic power.

Once my students assimilate the basic information, talk quickly turns to whether there will be more attacks, and if so, where they will be. I work hard to assuage their fears that our school or downtown Boston might be a target. After further conversation, we're called to the library, and with some relief I then send the class off to science and then lunch.

When they return to me for the last period of the day, our conversation turns to who would have done this and why. "I bet George Bush is behind this," Laquita declares. "I bet he did this so he could have an excuse to go to war with Iraq."

"What?!?!" I respond. "We don't know who's done this, but I can promise you it's not George Bush."

"No, Dr. Levinson, I think you're wrong," says Travis. "Bush doesn't care about anybody except rich people, and he wants to go to war with Iraq to take revenge for what Saddam Hussein did to his dad. President Bush probably got somebody to do this for him, like Laquita said."

More voices chime in to back Laquita up. Bush has the power to do something like this because he's the president. You know that he doesn't care about the law because he stole the whole election. All he wants to do is go to war with Iraq, and this is the perfect excuse. People in power can do anything and get away with it; look how his brother managed to keep black people from voting in Florida, and you don't see anything happening to him, do you? Bush is a horrible man—why wouldn't *he do something like this?*

I'm completely taken aback. Up until now, I've taken my students' questions in stride: their ignorance about the Pentagon, their confusion about the relationship between Manhattan and New York, their fears that our school would be the next target of attack. But this vitriol against President Bush, and their almost sanguine assumption that the president of the United States might choose to and be capable of killing five thousand, maybe ten thousand, American citizens simply on a whim—I find it breathtaking in its combination of utter ignorance and absolute cynicism.

My friends and family generally agreed with my assessment of my students' reactions—that they betrayed stunning cynicism and ignorance—when I began telling stories about my class soon after the September 11th attacks. How could they believe an American president could do this? my friends would ask. And how could they never have heard of the Pentagon? A number of people asked me if my students had confused the current President Bush with his father, and I answered no; they clearly distinguished between the two, and they knew that Hussein had been attacked by, and had tried to assassinate, Bush 41 rather than Bush 43. But nonetheless, I too felt that my students must have gotten confused somewhere along the way—and that their mistrust of "the system" was almost pathetic in its casualness.

In contrast, nowadays when I tell this story, people comment on my students' prescience. Instead of questioning their understanding of the distinction between the two President Bushes, listeners to my story question whether my students really could have made the claims I ascribe to them. Could they really have seen so far into the future, when none of the pundits in late 2001 and early 2002 did not? How could they have known, on September 11th, that President Bush would use these attacks to justify going to war against Iraq and deposing Saddam Hussein? My students were brilliant! Also, people point out, although it is too bad that my students had not heard of the Pentagon and did not know that Manhattan was a borough of New York City, there is little reason to think that the average white, middle-class, native-born eighth grader would have known this information either. Maybe the teachers in Arlington or Medford (two white, working- and middle-class suburbs of Boston) had to explain these things to their students, as well.

The latter point is well-taken, but I am not yet convinced that my students were so brilliant. Despite such profoundly troubling elements as President Bush's use of the September 11th attacks to justify what I believe to be a profoundly misguided war in Iraq, as well as his own deeply cynical and manipulative disinformation campaign to convince the American people that Saddam Hussein was a terrorist connected with the events of September 11th who posed an imminent threat to the United States; despite the Patriot Act's continuing threat to free speech, the White House's assault on due process for detainees at Guantanamo Bay and cavalier dismissal of the Geneva Convention; and despite the mounting evidence of the White House's complicity in torturing and killing Iraqi, Afghani, and other prisoners—despite all of these considerations, I still do not believe that President George W. Bush planned and executed the September 11th attacks on New York City and Washington, DC.

Why do I refuse to believe that President Bush could do something like this? So far as I am concerned, the facts do not bear out an alternative interpretation. But it is certainly plausible that I read the facts as I do in part because of my personal experience growing up and living as a white, middle-class, native-born American citizen. I have generally been well served by the United States: by its institutions, opportunities, freedoms, civil and public servants, class structure, and racial hierarchies. By contrast, why did so many of my students immediately assume that President Bush could have planned and executed the attacks? Again, so far as they were concerned, it is because facts such as the stolen 2000 election and the history of white, wealthy politicians holding ruthlessly onto power easily bore out their interpretation. But it is also certainly plausible that my students read the facts as they did because of their experiences growing up as non-white, poor, first- and second-generation immigrants in *de facto* segregated neighborhoods and schools. Growing up in poverty, vulnerable to violence and drugs, used to mutually mistrustful interactions with government representatives, labeled as "failures" by many people in power, and surrounded at home and in school entirely by others living in the same situation, my students have not always been well served by the United States. While in school, too, they learn about the depredations of American history and American presidents: President Andrew Jackson's contributions to the genocide of Native Americans, or President Abraham Lincoln's professed willingness to preserve the Union at the cost of maintaining slavery. Small wonder they interpret breaking news in such a way that implicates President Bush for complicity in the tragedy.

Whether my students are sadly ignorant or presciently brilliant, whether their life experiences blind or expose them to the true character of our political leaders, there is ample evidence that they are unlikely to become active participants in American civic and political life—and hence, that they are unlikely to influence civic and political deliberation or decision making. There is a profound *civic achievement gap*—as large and as disturbing as the reading and math achievement gaps that have received significant national attention in recent years—between poor, ethnic/racial minority, and immigrant citizens, on the one hand, and middle-class, white, and native-born citizens, on the other. Although statistics are not destiny, it is extremely likely that my students at McCormack will vote, contribute time and money to political campaigns, contact government officials, and even attend protests at much lower rates than their white, middle-class counterparts attending schools just a few miles away.

What can schools like McCormack do to help the overwhelmingly poor and minority students who attend them to become civically engaged and politically empowered? To what extent does an effective civic education in these schools need to take into account these students' life experiences, readings of history, and interpretations of current events? If these do turn out to be significant, what does this imply about the construction of American citizenship more generally? These are the questions that motivate this essay.

The Civic Achievement Gap and *De Facto* Segregated Schools

Good citizens possess and exhibit a wide range of civic *knowledge, skills, attitudes,* and *behaviors.* Good citizens need to be knowledgeable about politics, history, government, and current events. They need to be skilled communicators, thinkers, and deliberators. They need to be concerned about the common good in addition to their own self-interest and to believe it is possible and worth trying to make a difference through public action. Citizens also need to become involved in public or community affairs, through some combination of voting, protesting, contacting public officials, mobilizing others, contributing time or money to causes or campaigns, participating in community groups, and other appropriate actions.

On all of these measures, there is evidence of a profound *civic achievement gap* between poor, minority, and immigrant youth and adults, on the one hand, and middle-class or wealthy, white, and native-born youth and adults, on the other. For example:

Knowledge and Skills. As early as the fourth grade, African American, Hispanic, and poor students perform worse on the civics test of the National Assessment of Educational Progress (NAEP) than white, Asian, and middle-class students. American ninth graders' scores showed similar race- and income-dependent disparities on a recent IEA international test of civic knowledge and skills. Among adults, similarly, "men are more informed than women; whites are more informed than blacks; those with higher incomes are more informed than those with lower incomes; and older citizens are more informed than younger ones."

Behavior/Participation. In the presidential election of 2000, Hispanic and Asian voting-age citizens voted at a rate only two-thirds that of eligible whites, while poor people voted at barely half the rate of middle-class and wealthy people. First- and second-generation immigrant citizens also voted at significantly lower rates than native-born citizens. Gaps in participation rates go well beyond voting. People who earn over $75,000 annually are politically active at up to *six times* the rate of people who earn under $15,000, whether measured by working for a campaign, serving on the board of an organization, or even such relatively low-cost actions as participating in protests or contacting officials. Similarly, Hispanics are less politically involved than whites and blacks according to a wide variety of measures. Hispanic young adults (ages eighteen to twenty-four) in particular have much lower rates of community involvement than their white and black peers.

Attitudes. For both youth and adults, race and class correlate with huge gaps—"chasms," in the words of scholars Robert Smith and Richard Seltzer—in their trust in government, trust in each other, and sense of political efficacy. The poorest individuals, for instance, express political interest and political efficacy at levels almost a full standard deviation lower than the wealthiest. These differences can be profound across racial groups: in a study of individuals' responses to the 2000 presidential election voting irregularities in Florida, for example, nearly one-fifth of African American survey respondents interpreted the "problems with the ballots or voting machines" as being "a deliberate attempt to reduce the political power of minorities," whereas barely 1–3 percent of white, Asian, and Hispanic survey respondents felt the same way.

These ethnoracial-, class-, and immigration-based disparities in political knowledge, skills, attitudes, and involvement are neither morally acceptable nor politically tenable to maintain a legitimate democratic system. One can draw this conclusion even if one is not an egalitarian. In fact, anyone who believes in the value of democratic governance should recognize how crucial it is to narrow the civic achievement gap. Civic knowledge, skills, and attitudes profoundly influence civic and political behavior. Civic and political engagement, concomitantly, are central to the strength, stability, and legitimacy of democracy. Studies confirm that civic knowledge is clearly and directly correlated with higher levels of political participation and expressions of democratic values such as tolerance, stable political attitudes, and the adoption of "enlightened self-interest." Mastery of civic skills is also tied to both the likelihood and effectiveness of civic participation. Participation, of course, matters because democratic governance relies on participatory citizens. The legitimacy, stability, and quality of democratic regimes are all directly dependent on the robust participation of a representative and large cross section of citizens. Attitudes matter, finally, because they constitute the motivational preconditions for civic engagement. Empirical research has shown that political efficacy, civic duty, and civic identity are all crucial for motivating civic and political engagement. In sum, the civic achievement gap is a significant and documentable threat to democratic ideals and practice. It is important for both the civic and political empowerment of poor, minority, and immigrant individuals, and for the health of the polity as a whole, that we develop a means of closing the gap.

One important battleground for attacking the civic achievement gap is the network of mostly urban schools that serve a *de facto* segregated, poor, minority, and immigrant student population. Fully one-third of black and Latino students in the United States, and over half of the black students in the Northeast, attend schools that have a 90-100 percent minority student population. The overwhelming majority of these schools are in urban areas, often in central cities. Over half of all schools in the hundred largest school districts are 81–100 percent minority; among these one hundred districts, public schools in Los Angeles, Houston, Detroit, Dallas, Santa Ana, Atlanta, San Antonio, Oakland, and Washington, DC, all had a minority student population above 90 percent in 2000–2001, which means in practice that most schools had a virtually 100 percent minority population. The students in these schools and districts are also generally poor. Over half the students in the hundred largest school districts are eligible for free or reduced-price lunch, and in sixteen of these districts, including the three largest in the country (New York City, Los Angeles, and Puerto Rico, which together account for over 2 million students), more than seven out of every ten students are eligible for free or reduced-price lunch. Finally, it is worth noting that schools are continuing to resegregate, and the public and political will to press for integrated schools is diminishing in the United States. Hence, not only do a large number of poor, ethnically, or racially segregated public schools currently exist and educate a substantial percentage of ethnic and racial minority students in the United States, but if anything, their numbers are likely to increase rather than decrease over the coming years, especially as the minority population in the United States also grows. Consequently, if we care about political stability, democratic legitimacy, and civic equality then we must care about what gets taught and learned in these schools—not just for the students' sakes but for our own, as well.

Reformulating Civic Education within the Social Studies: Students' Construction of Civic Narrative

How can *de facto* segregated, poor, and minority schools help reduce the civic achievement gap, and hence promote true civic and political equality for all Americans? First, civic education must be restored to the curriculum. There has been a precipitous decline in the number, range, and frequency of civics courses offered in US elementary and high schools, and this decline needs to be reversed. Second, social studies education needs to be constructivist rather than delivery-oriented. Since students are constructing their own historical understanding anyway, the school should be an empowering partner in this process rather than a passive bystander or worse, a mistrusted hindrance. Third, civic education must become experiential. Students—especially poor, minority, and immigrant students growing up and attending schools in predominantly poor, minority, or immigrant communities— need to *experience*, not just read about, meaningful and successful civic and political participation. Finally, schools need to be explicit about both the impediments faced by and the opportunities available to poor, minority, and immigrant youth in the United States, and they need to teach students specific techniques for overcoming these impediments. Taken together, these reforms will reduce the civic achievement gap by enabling all students to construct civic narratives that simultane- ously "keep it real" and incorporate positive, forward-looking atti- tudes that promote high levels of civic knowledge, skills, and actual engagement.

1. Restore civic education to the curriculum. First, the civic achievement gap will never be reduced unless we actually start teach- ing civics again in our public schools. One finds ample evidence that civic education improves civic outcomes, but instructional time, finan- cial resources, and professional development for civic education have dropped markedly over the past thirty or forty years—especially in schools serving minority students. In the 1960s, students regularly took as many as three civics courses in high school, including civics, democ- racy, and government; now students tend to take only one—govern- ment—and that only in the twelfth grade, by which point many poor and minority students have, sadly, already dropped out. The national emphasis on reading, mathematics, and eventually science motivated by the No Child Left Behind Act of 2001 is also threatening further to reduce the attention paid to social studies. A recent survey by the Council for Basic Education showed that almost half of the principals in high-minority elementary schools reported reducing the amount of social studies instructional time since 2000 in deference to the need to increase student achievement in reading, writing, math, and science. In my own school this year, students take social studies for only a semes- ter instead of the entire school year because of increased time spent on

English and math. Happily, this trend has not yet afflicted most high schools. If we want to narrow the civic achievement gap, though, especially by increasing civic knowledge and skills of poor, minority, and immigrant students, then civic education must begin in elementary schools and be a regular part of education K-12 (and beyond).

2. **Teach a constructivist curriculum.** In addition to increasing the *quantity* of civic education in the formal curriculum, we also need to increase its *quality*, specifically by teaching social studies in such a way that students are enabled to construct empowering civic narratives that simultaneously cohere with their lived experiences and impel them to civic and political action. This requires an enormous shift in the social studies curriculum delivery model that one finds in most American schools (especially urban schools) today. As their responses on September 11th demonstrated, students do not enter the classroom as blank slates, willing to accept whatever story about American politics, government, and opportunity that schools try to teach. Rather, they come in with views of their own, gleaned from family, neighbors, community leaders, the media, and probably most importantly, their own direct experiences. Although I failed to be sufficiently impressed with this at the time (shocked as I was by their ready assumption that President Bush had ordered the mass murder of American citizens), my students readily incorporated both their own experiences of disenfranchisement and their understanding of history, including the Florida election controversy, Saddam Hussein's attempt on the first President Bush's life, and the Persian Gulf War (which ended before most of them had turned four), into their interpretation of current events—all without any adult guidance or encouragement.

Hence, social studies teachers need to be responsive to students' construction of historical and civic knowledge and need to provide students opportunities to acquire knowledge, develop skills, and practice behaviors that will enable students both to construct and to enact a more empowering story about their role within the polity. One means of accomplishing this is to teach history as a dialogue between the past and the present, explicitly acknowledging but also modeling for students how our understanding of the past shapes our views of the present and vice versa. Only by explicitly engaging students' use of the past and present ("White people would still have us in slavery if they could." "Nobody could've kept me in slavery! I would have just stolen a gun and shot my owner, 'blam, blam!', and been out of there!") can teachers and schools hope to help students construct more sophisticated, nuanced, and potentially empowering conceptions of their potential roles within the United States. Furthermore, this historical dialogue needs to be open to multiple contemporary interpretations. It must incorporate not only many "voices of the past," which is well accepted by now, but also permit many "present voices" to construct a *variety* of American stories, rather than "the American story" as is favored by some contemporary educators, historians, and politicians.

3. Incorporate experiential education. In order further to change their minds about the opportunities provided by civic and political engagement, and not just focus on the impediments or even dangers, we need to give students positive, real-world civic and political experiences. Experiential civic education can take a multiplicity of forms, including activities within classrooms and schools as well as those beyond school walls. Students may serve on the school council, governing board, or diversity committee. They may invite local community leaders to visit the school and then interview them about their accomplishments, the challenges they face, and what motivates them to keep on working for what they believe in. After conducting a "constituent survey" of their peers, students may develop and implement a strategy to improve the quality of food in the school cafeteria. Students may debate current events and then write letters expressing their opinions to an elected representative or government official. They can participate in a mock trial, conduct a voter registration drive in the school parking lot or before PTA meetings, or create a Web site about a policy issue that matters to them. An ambitious teacher may encourage students to volunteer with a nonprofit social services agency or an advocacy organization and prepare a PowerPoint presentation about what makes it an effective (or ineffective) organization. Similarly ambitiously, students may research a public policy issue and then make a presentation to local officials or attend a city council meeting as advocates for their position. Or, closer to home, they can elect class officers who will collaborate with the teacher on planning field trips and other special activities; or, they may as a class deliberate about and vote on such issues as the due dates for major projects, the order in which to read class novels, or the consequences for minor disciplinary infractions.

Research uniformly supports the efficacy of these kinds of active civic learning approaches. Done well, experiential civic education helps students learn and apply a significant amount of civic knowledge, develop a number of civic skills, embrace positive civic attitudes, and practice important civic behaviors. It promotes an active, explicitly political conception of citizenship. It can help students make contacts with adults and role models in the community, as well as help the participating organizations and institutions themselves. Experiential civic education can motivate students to become civically engaged in the future by contributing to their sense of empowerment and agency, connecting them to adults and peers who model civically engaged behavior, and enabling them to use their knowledge and skills to achieve concrete results. Experiential civic education may also reinforce (or generate) adults' sense of connection to, and responsibility and respect for, the younger generation, including toward children and young adults who live and are being educated in communities very different from those of the adults. These are all extremely important civic outcomes.

Experiential education also does not require elaborate field trips or mammoth projects to be effective. Although such projects are certainly possible, it is also relatively easy to give students the opportunity to exercise and reflect on their democratic rights and responsibilities, and to experience making a positive difference, entirely within the school walls and the school day. More than half of the examples I gave above, for instance, require nothing more than access to current news sources and a teacher and school culture that supports student experimentation in democratic participation. Furthermore, many projects require no increase in instructional time, and many can be implemented in classes other than social studies with little or no loss of content.

It is important to note, however, that all of the examples I gave intentionally built on collective and policy-oriented action. There were no piecemeal approaches of donating cans to a homeless shelter or spending a morning visiting elderly people in a nursing home. Although such activities are noble and worthwhile, they do not foster attention to systemic issues and they do not help students recognize the power of their community and of joining together to effect change.

4. Teach explicit strategies for empowerment. This emphasis on collective action's empowerment of poor, minority, historically disenfranchised group members brings us to my final point. Schools need to be forthright with students both about the opportunities they have and the obstacles they face, and they also must teach students the skills that will help them overcome these obstacles. These skills include the ability to speak Standard American English at appropriate times, to dress according to mainstream norms (no baggy pants or do-rags when talking to a city councilor), and to interact in ways that accord with the cultural practices of those in power. Looking a city councilor in the eye when speaking to her, for example, is crucial but contrary to how my African American students in Atlanta and my Vietnamese students in Boston have been taught by their families to show respect. Teachers and schools can teach such skills in ways that demonstrate respect for students' own cultural traditions and community norms while simultaneously imparting the knowledge and skills necessary for broader civic and political empowerment.

As schools put these reforms into place—increasing instructional time and other resources for civic education, helping students construct multiple historical narratives, implementing experiential civic education, and teaching students civic and political strategies for empowerment—they will provide students with a set of empowering civic experiences that are likely to increase their sense of political efficacy and civic identity, and hence to inspire their acquisition of civic knowledge and skills as well as continued productive participation.

There is no doubt that the reforms I propose face impediments. Schools, especially those that serve predominantly minority, poor, or immigrant students and have a history of low test scores, will continue to feel pressure to focus on reading, math, and possibly science, to the exclusion of civic education. These schools are also the least likely to be self-governing, since many are part of large urban systems subject to both bureaucratic and union regulations, and they are also more likely to have large student bodies. Both conditions make it hard to create opportunities for widespread student democratic participation in school governance. Finally, many school administrators and teachers may be concerned that experiential civic education has the potential to foster partisanship, and they may hence worry about bringing up or involving students in controversial issues.

Although these concerns are valid and important, they are not dispositive. Experiential education can energize student learning in many areas—including in math and reading. Preparing a speech to deliver to the school board or analyzing a budget in an attempt to improve the cafeteria food can profoundly motivate students to develop and apply communication and math skills. In addition, it is worth remembering that experiential civic education can be built into the school day; hence it need not distract from other subjects.

Furthermore, even the most regulated schools can create pockets of control to be exercised jointly by adults and students in the school building. And finally, although schools should be worried about *partisanship*, they should not avoid touching on *politics*, which is central to civic engagement: with thoughtfulness and care, teachers and administrators can distinguish between what is political and what is partisan and engage their students in the former without running afoul of the latter.

The value of reducing the civic achievement gap, and thereby of civically and politically empowering poor, minority, and immigrant students, is hard to overstate. In addition to empowering the students themselves, schools will help strengthen local communities, both via the direct work that students accomplish and by building a new generation of mobilized, empowered adults. Reducing the civic achievement gap also strengthens democracy. It broadens government representation, increases its responsiveness to diverse individuals and communities, and thereby also reinforces its political legitimacy in the eyes of historically disenfranchised community members. Reducing the civic achievement gap strengthens schools, as students turn their attention to solving problems collaboratively as opposed to fighting against the system or just checking out. And finally, it promotes civic and political equality and fairness—ideals that are central to our American democracy. These are goals all schools can and should embrace.

This chapter appeared previously in *Philosophy & Public Policy Quarterly*, vol. 25, no. 1/2 (Winter/Spring 2005).

Sources

All names of students have been changed to protect their privacy. I discussed my students' response to the September 11th attacks with a few African American friends and colleagues; they were both less surprised by and less critical of my students than I. They, too, however, were unconvinced by my students' claim that President Bush himself had ordered the attack. In retrospect, they tended to agree more with Walter Mosley's recent comment in the *New York Times Magazine:* "I have never met an African-American who was surprised by the attack on the World Trade Center. Blacks do not see America as the great liberator of the world. Blacks understand how the rest of the world sees us, because we have also been the victims of American imperialism." This quote appears in Deborah Solomon, "Questions for Walter Mosley: It's the Money, Stupid," *New York Times Magazine*, 17 (2004). Information on race-, income-, and gender-correlated differences in civic knowledge can be found in Anthony D. Lutkus, Andrew R. Weiss, Jay R. Campbell, John Mazzeo, and Stephen Lazer, *NAEP 1998 Civics Report Card for the Nation* (Washington, DC, US Department of Education, Office of Educational Research and Improvement, and National Center for Education Statistics, 1999). Statistics about different rates of civic participation can be found in *Voting and Registration in the Election of November* (Washington, DC, US Census Bureau, 2002), Mark Hugo Lopez, *Electoral Engagement Among Latino Youth* (CIRCLE, 2003) and Sidney Verba, Kay Lehman Schlozman, and Henry E. Brady, *Voice and Equality: Civic Voluntarism in American Politics* (Cambridge, MA, Harvard Univ. Press, 1995). Robert Smith and Richard Seltzer discuss the "chasm" in race-correlated political attitudes in their book *Contemporary Controversies and the American Racial Divide* (Lanham, MD, Rowman and Littlefield, 2000). Information on the point that the poorest individuals express political interest and political efficacy at levels almost a full standard deviation lower than the wealthiest is found in the Verba, Schlozman, and Brady volume. Information regarding the response to the 2000 presidential election voting irregularities in Florida is found in *Race and Ethnicity in 2001: Attitudes, Perceptions, and Experiences*, sponsored by the *Washington Post*, the Kaiser Family Foundation, and Harvard University (Washington, DC, 2001). The adoption of "enlightened self-interest" is discussed by, among others, William A. Galston, "Political Knowledge, Political Engagement, and Civic Education," *Annual Reviews Political Science*, vol. 4 (2001) and Michael Delli Carpini and Scott Keeter, *What Americans Know about Politics and Why It Matters* (New Haven, CT, Yale Univ. Press, 1997). Data on the majority minority population of urban schools are found in Gary Orfield, *Schools More Separate: Consequences of a Decade of Resegregation* (Cambridge, MA, The Civil Rights Project, Harvard Univ., 2001) and also Gary Orfield, Susan Eaton, and The Harvard Project on Desegregation, *Dismantling Desegregation: The Quiet Reversal of Brown v. Board of Education* (New York, The New Press, 1996). Data regarding the minority population in schools in large American cities (and in Puerto Rico) are found in: US Department of Education and National Center for Education Statistics, *Characteristics of the 100 Largest Public Elementary and Secondary School Districts in the United States: 2000-01* (Washington, DC, National Center for Education Statistics, 2002), especially Tables 8 and 9. For data that civic education improves civic outcomes, see the Delli Carpini and Keeter work; Richard D. Niemi and Jane Junn, *Civic Education: What Makes Students Learn* (New Haven, CT, Yale Univ. Press, 1998); William Damon, "To Not Fade Away: Restoring Civil Identity among the

Young," in *Making Good Citizens,* edited by Diane Ravitch and Joseph P. Viteritti (New Haven, CT, Yale Univ. Press, 2001); William A. Galston's 2001 work; Judith Torney-Purta, "The School's Role in Developing Civic Engagement: A Study of Adolescents in Twenty-Eight Countries," *Applied Developmental Science,* vol. 6 (2002); Judith Torney-Purta, Carole L. Hahn, and Jo-Ann M. Amadeo, "Principles of Subject-Specific Instruction in Education for Citizenship," in *Subject-Specific Instructional Methods and Activities,* edited by Jere Brophy (New York, JAI Press, 2001); and Carnegie Corporation of New York and CIRCLE, *The Civic Mission of Schools* (New York, Carnegie Corporation of New York and CIRCLE, 2003). The point that in the 1960s students took as many as three civics courses in high school but now students tend to take only one is made by Niemi and Junn (1998) and the Carnegie Corporation of New York and CIRCLE work of 2003. For a discussion of principals reducing social studies instructional time, see Claus von Zastrow, *Academic Atrophy: The Condition of the Liberal Arts in America's Public Schools* (Washington, DC, Council for Basic Education, 2004). For a discussion of historical dialogue needing to be open to multiple contemporary interpretations, see Albert Shanker Institute, *Education for Democracy* (Washington, DC, Albert Shanker Institute, 2003). For discussions of kinds of active civic learning approaches, see Carole L. Hahn, *Becoming Political* (Albany, State Univ. of New York Press, 1998); Jo-Ann Amadeo, Judith Torney-Purta, Rainer Lehmann, Vera Husfeldt, and Roumiana Nikolova, *Civic Knowledge and Engagement: An IEA Study of Upper Secondary Students in Sixteen Countries, Executive Summary* (Amsterdam, IEA and the Carnegie Corporation of New York, 2002) and the CIRCLE work of 2003. For a discussion of interactions that follow the practices of those in power, see Lisa Delpit, *Other People's Children* (New York, The New Press, 1995).

Civic Education and Political Participation

William A. Galston

Anxiety about the civic attitudes and activities of young adults in America is nothing new, and its persistence is easy to understand. As far back as evidence can be found—and virtually without exception—young adults seem to have been less attached to civic life than their parents and grandparents. Nor is it difficult to find plausible explanations for this gap. Civic attachment is linked to such factors as professional interests (and self-interests), a stable residential location, home ownership, marriage, and parenthood, all of which are statistically less characteristic of younger adults. Not surprisingly, in every generation the simple passage of time has brought maturing young adults more fully into the circle of civic life. So are today's worries any more justified than in times past? Has anything changed?

The answer, I believe, is yes. The reason is to be found in the demographic distinction between cohort effects and generational effects. "Cohorts" represent a snapshot of different age groups at the same historical moment, while "generations" represent the same age groups at different historical moments. If we compare generations rather than cohorts—that is, if we compare today's young adults not with today's older adults but with young adults of the past—we find evidence of diminished civic attachment.

Some of the basic facts are well known. In the early 1970s, about one-half of eighteen- to twenty-nine-year-olds voted in presidential elections. By 2000, fewer than one-third did. The same pattern holds for congressional elections—a bit more than one-fourth in the mid-1970s, compared to less than one-fifth in 2002.

Less well-known are the trends charted by a remarkable UCLA study, conducted since the mid-1960s and involving 250,000 matriculating college freshmen each year. Over this period, every significant indicator of political engagement has fallen by about half. Only 33 percent of freshmen think that keeping up with politics is important, down from 60 percent in 1966 (though up a bit from the all-time low of 28 percent recorded in 2000). Only 16 percent say they frequently discuss politics, down from 33 percent in 1966. Not surprisingly, acquisition of political knowledge from traditional media sources is way down, and as yet not enough young people are using the Internet to fill the role newspapers and network TV news once played as sources of civic information.

But the news is not all bad by any means. Today's young people are patriotic, tolerant, and compassionate. They believe in America's principles and in the American Dream. They adeptly navigate our nation's increasing diversity. And, as has been widely reported and discussed, they are more than willing to give of themselves to others. College freshmen are reporting significantly increased levels of volunteering in their last year of high school, a trend that seems to be carrying over to their early college years. But only one-third of today's young volunteers believe that they will continue this practice once they enter the paid work force. And there is no evidence that such volunteerism will lead to wider civic engagement.

On the contrary, young people typically characterize their volunteering as an *alternative* to official politics, which they see as self-absorbed and unrelated to their deeper ideals. They have limited knowledge of government's impact, either on themselves or on those they seek to assist. They understand why it matters to feed a hungry person at a soup kitchen; they do not understand why it matters where government sets eligibility levels for food stamps or payment levels for the Earned Income Tax Credit. They have confidence in personalized acts with consequences they can see for themselves; they have less confidence in collective actions (especially those undertaken through public institutions), whose consequences they see as remote, opaque, and impossible to control.

I do not intend this as a reproach. The blame (if that is an appropriate characterization at all) rightly attaches to older adults, who have failed in their responsibility to transmit workable civic norms; to provide practical contexts in which young people can develop civic knowledge, dispositions, and skills; and to conduct our politics in a manner that engages young people's aspirations and ideals. The surge of patriotic sentiment among young people in the immediate wake of September 11th has not yielded a comparable surge in engaged, active citizenship. And I am not alone in tracing this gap to the failure of our public institutions to offer enough meaningful venues for young people to put their civic impulses into practice. What is true of most people is especially true for young people: we tend to respond to concrete challenges and opportunities, in the absence of which we may not be motivated to translate our good intentions into action.

Why Does Civic Disengagement Matter?

I believe that the increasing civic detachment of the young cannot be regarded with equanimity. First, let me offer a truism about representative democracy: political engagement is necessary but not sufficient for political effectiveness. If today's young people have legitimate generational interests that do not wholly coincide with the interests of their elders, then those interests cannot shape public decisions unless they are forcefully articulated. We should be debating higher education finance, job training, and family policy as vigorously as we do the future of Social Security and Medicare. We aren't, and we won't, unless younger Americans become more engaged. The withdrawal of a cohort of citizens from public affairs disturbs the balance of public deliberation to the detriment of those who withdraw (and of many others besides).

Second, I would offer an old-fashioned argument from obligation. Most young Americans derive great benefits from their membership in a stable, prosperous, and free society. These goods do not fall like manna from heaven; they must be produced and renewed by each generation. Every citizen has a moral responsibility to contribute his or her fair share to sustaining the public institutions and processes on which we all depend and from which we all benefit.

Third, I come to the relation between citizenship and self-development. Even if we agree (and we may not) on the activities that constitute good citizenship, one may still wonder why it is good to be a good citizen. After all, it is possible for many individuals to realize their good in ways that do not involve the active exercise of citizenship. Even if we accept

Aristotle's characterization of politics as the architectonic activity, it does not follow that the development of civic capacities is architectonic for every soul.

Still, there is something to the proposition that, under appropriate circumstances, political engagement helps develop capacities that are intrinsically important. I have in mind the sorts of intellectual and moral capacities that de Tocqueville and Mill discuss or gesture toward: among them enlarged interests, a wider human sympathy, a sense of active responsibility for oneself, the skills needed to work with others toward goods that can only be obtained through collective action, and the powers of sympathetic understanding needed to build bridges of persuasive words to those with whom one must act.

These links between participation and character development are empirical, not theoretical, propositions, and we do not yet have the kind of evidence we need to sustain them against doubt. On the other hand, we do not have compelling reasons to doubt them, and we can at least advance them as a plausible profession of public faith—as long as we are not too categorical about it.

It may well be that, even as civic engagement has declined, it has become not less but more necessary for the development of the human capacities just sketched. Underlying this conjecture is the suspicion that, as the market has become more pervasive during the past generation as organizing metaphor and as daily experience, the range of opportunities to develop nonmarket skills and dispositions has narrowed. For various reasons, the solidaristic organizations that dominated the US landscape from the 1930s through the early 1960s have weakened, and the principle of individual choice has emerged as our central value. Indeed, citizenship itself has become optional, as the sense of civic obligation (to vote or to do anything else of civic consequence) has faded and as the military draft has been replaced by all-volunteer armed forces. When the chips are down, we prefer exit to voice, and any sense of loyalty to something larger than ourselves has all but disappeared. In this context, the experience of collective action directed toward common purposes is one of the few conceivable counterweights to today's hyperextended principle of individual choice.

If civic engagement is more necessary than ever, our manifest failure to foster it among young adults looms all the larger. The formative mechanisms and mobilizing arenas of civic opportunity are many. For example, evidence presented in *The Civic Mission of Schools*, a national report jointly produced by the Carnegie Corporation and the Center for Information and Research on Civic Learning and Engagement (CIRCLE) and made public earlier this year, demonstrates the impact of parents and faith-based institutions on the civic life of young people. In the remainder of this article, I will focus on the most traditional of these mechanisms and opportunities—our public schools—and on the most old-fashioned of their efforts to encourage political engagement: namely, civic education.

The Current Failure of Civic Education

The evidence that we have failed to transmit basic civic knowledge to young adults is now incontrovertible. In our decentralized system of public education, the closest thing we have to a national examination is the National Assessment of Educational Progress (NAEP), which is devised by teams of subject-matter experts and then carefully field-tested and revised in a process directed by the National Assessment Governing Board. The NAEP is administered biennially in what are deemed "core academic subjects." Unfortunately, civic education has not yet achieved that exalted status, and we are fortunate if civic knowledge is assessed once a decade. For each subject, four different achievement levels are defined: "below basic," which means little if any demonstrated knowledge of the subject, "basic," which indicates partial mastery; "proficient," which is the level representing a standard of adequate knowledge; and "advanced." These achievement levels represent absolute thresholds, not percentiles. In principle, every student could reach the level of proficiency.

The results of the most recent NAEP Civics Assessment were released three years ago. They were not encouraging. For fourth-, eighth-, and (most relevant for our purposes) twelfth-graders, about three-fourths were below the level of proficiency. Thirty-five percent of high school seniors tested below basic, indicating near-total civic ignorance. Another 39 percent were at the basic level, demonstrating less than the working knowledge that citizens need.

When we combine these NAEP results with other data from the past decade of survey research, we are driven to a gloomy conclusion: whether we are concerned with the rules of the political game, political players, domestic policy, foreign policy, or political geography, student performance is quite low. And this is puzzling. While the level of formal schooling in the United States is much higher than it was fifty years ago, the civic knowledge of today's students is no higher than that of their parents and grandparents. We have made a major investment in formal education, without any discernible payoff in increased civic knowledge.

Several state-by-state analyses of civic education, the most recent of which, *Educating Democracy: State Standards to Ensure a Civic Core,* was released by the Albert Shanker Institute in the spring of 2003, help explain these unimpressive results. While most states endorse civic education in their constitutions and declaratory policies, only half the states have even partially specified a required core of civic knowledge, fewer have made a serious effort to align their civics-related courses with challenging standards, and only a handful administer exams focused exclusively on civic topics. In many states, certification requirements do not ensure that teachers called upon to teach civics will have the education and training needed to do the job. Other studies indicate that a significant percentage of history and social studies teachers, who typically end up leading civics classes, have little formal preparation for that task (or indeed for teaching history and social studies).

In addition, school-based civic education has been in decline over the past three decades. According to *The Civic Mission of Schools,* most high school civic education today consists of a single government course, compared with the three courses in civics, democracy, and government that were common until the 1960s. Unlike the traditional civics course, today's government class analyzes and describes politics as a distant subject matter, often with little explicit discussion of citizens' rights and responsibilities. Nor is the decline limited to high school. In just one decade, between 1988 and 1998, the proportion of fourth-graders who reported taking social studies daily fell steeply from 49 percent to only 39 percent.

The causes of this decline are multiple and not easily summarized. Let me mention just two. First, many teachers, principals, and school boards fear criticism—or even litigation—if they address topics that some parents or other members of the community may consider inappropriately controversial or political. In response, many school systems have backed away from civic education. Second, the push for high-stakes testing in core academic subjects can come at the expense of subjects not considered to be part of the core, as civics usually is not.

Does Civic Knowledge Matter?

It is easy to dismiss these findings as irrelevant to the broader concerns with which I began. Who cares whether young people master the boring content of civics courses? Why does it matter whether they can identify their representatives or name the branches of government? Surprisingly, recent research documents important links between basic civic information and civic attributes that we have good reason to care about.

- Civic knowledge promotes support for democratic values. The more knowledge we have of the workings of government, the more likely we are to support the core values of democratic self-government, starting with tolerance.
- Civic knowledge promotes political participation. All other things being equal, the more knowledge people have, the more likely they are to participate in civic and political affairs.
- Civic knowledge helps citizens to understand their interests as individuals and as members of groups. There is a rational relationship between one's interests and particular legislation: the more knowledge we have, the more readily and accurately we connect with and defend our interests in the political process.
- Civic knowledge helps citizens learn more about civic affairs. Unless we have a certain core of knowledge, it is difficult to acquire more knowledge. Moreover, the new knowledge we do gain can be used effectively only if we are able to integrate it into an existing framework.
- The more knowledge we have of civic affairs, the less we have a sort of generalized mistrust and fear of public life. Ignorance is the father of fear, and knowledge is the mother of trust.
- Civic knowledge improves the consistency of citizens' views as expressed on public opinion surveys. The more knowledge people have, the more consistent their view over time on political affairs. This does not mean that people do not change their views, but it does mean that they know their own minds.
- Civic knowledge can alter our opinion on specific civic issues. For example, the more civic knowledge people have, the less likely they are to fear new immigrants and their impact on our country.

Doing School-Based Civic Education

As recently as a decade ago, the conventional wisdom (backed by academic research from the 1970s) was that school-based civic education was doomed to ineffectiveness. However, the most recent research points in a more optimistic direction. While there is no magic bullet, there are a number of effective approaches to civic education. *The Civic Mission of Schools* summarizes their shared characteristics as follows:

- a deliberate, intentional focus on civic outcomes, such as students' propensity to vote, to work on local problems, to join voluntary associations, and to follow the news;
- explicit advocacy of civic and political engagement, without advocating a particular position or partisan stance;
- active learning opportunities that offer students the chance to engage in discussions of relevant issues and to take part in activities that help put a "real-life" perspective on classroom learning; and
- an emphasis on the ideas and principles that are essential to constitutional democracy, such as those found in the Declaration of Independence and the US Constitution, and on how they influence education, religion, the workplace, and government at every level.

In addition, this report stressed the importance of school environment and culture to the acquisition of civic skills and attitudes. The most effective programs occur in schools that:

- consciously promote civic engagement by all students, with special attention to those who might otherwise remain disengaged;
- give students opportunities to contribute opinions about school governance—through student governments and other forums such as all-school assemblies and small working groups—and to understand how school systems are run;
- collaborate with the community and local institutions to provide civic learning opportunities;
- provide teachers with access to professional development in civic education; and
- infuse a civic mission throughout the curriculum, offer an array of extracurricular activities, and provide a school climate that helps students put what they learn about civic education and democracy into practice.

The Importance and the Challenge

While the importance of effective civic education is perennial, several trends combine to make it especially urgent today: the United States must integrate an unprecedented wave of immigrants into the mainstream of civic life; left unchecked, troubling inequalities in the civic participation of different socioeconomic and ethnic groups could exacerbate undesirable political and policy trends; and civic education is one of the few forces that can resist the rising tide of materialism in US culture that numerous surveys have documented.

The difficulty of this task at least matches its importance. Not only do community-level disagreements about controversial policies continue to pose problems for teachers and school administrators, but also, at a deeper level, Americans do not wholly agree about the kind of citizenship we want our schools to foster. The question we face is whether there is enough agreement on some basics to allow us to proceed in spite of these differences. The experience of recent efforts to find common ground, spearheaded by such groups as the Center for Civic Education, the National Commission on Civic Renewal, and the joint Carnegie/CIRCLE project, points in an encouraging direction. The ultimate test, however, will occur on the ground, if and when every state decides to address this challenge in a serious and sustained way.

This chapter first appeared in the *Phi Delta Kappan,* September 2003, and appears with the kind permission of that journal's editor.

Sources

Sources for the empirical claims made in this article include William A. Galston, "Political Knowledge, Political Engagement, and Civic Education," Annual Review of Political Science, vol. 4, 2001, pp. 217-34; the Carnegie Corporation of New York and the Center for Information and Research on Civic Learning and Engagement (CIRCLE), *The Civic Mission of Schools,* available at www.civicmissionof-schools.org; and fact sheets developed by CIRCLE, available at www.civicyouth.org.

The Challenge of Civic Debate

II

State Symbols and Multiculturalism

Jacob T. Levy

American voters and the American media paid renewed attention to the Confederate battle flag during the early months of 2000. The NAACP-organized boycott of South Carolina over that state's flying of the battle flag over its statehouse mixed with the Republican presidential primaries to send the flag issue into the headlines. In Texas, then-governor George W. Bush tried to rally conservative voters to help him shut down a challenge from Arizona Senator John McCain by insisting that the fate of the flag was a matter to be decided only by the people of South Carolina. McCain initially criticized the flag, then offered a stiff and formal endorsement of the purely-a-state-matter position. (After the primaries ended he admitted that the latter endorsement had been a lie.) McCain's own South Carolina campaign chair was a leading member of the so-called "Southern Heritage" movement, which is dedicated to celebrating the memory of the Confederacy. Along with Bob Jones University, the Confederate symbols and nostalgia dominated the national media's coverage of the primary and became a synecdoche for the story that South Carolina was politically extremist, backward, and bigoted. Eventually, in a compromise rejected by the NAACP, the Confederate flag was taken off the capitol building but transferred to another site on the capitol grounds. The long-running disputes over the battle flag continue. Georgia, for example, continues to include the battle flag as a portion of its official state flag, as it has since shortly after the US Supreme Court decided *Brown vs. Board of Education.*

Disputes Over Symbols

These ongoing disputes from across the South are echoed in the American West. Gerard Baker was the first American Indian to serve as National Parks Service superintendent of the Little Big Horn National Battlefield (renamed as such after being called the Custer National Battlefield from 1946 until 1991). His half-decade in that office ended in 1997 after he tired of near-constant conflict with enthusiasts for General George Armstrong Custer, whose forces were wiped out by a Sioux and Cheyenne army in 1876. The renaming was the first step in shifting the site away from a celebration of Custer toward a commemoration of those who died on both sides; the same bill also authorized a monument to the Indian dead to stand near the existing monument to Custer. Baker tried to push that process farther, allowing Indian rituals of remembrance to be practiced on the battlefield and overhauling the content of the site's tours and educational programs. The "Custer buffs" protested at every stage, insisting that the process was politically-correct pandering to an ethnic minority. (One supporter of the changes, US Representative Pat Williams of Montana, observed that "as far as we can tell, it was the only battlefield named after a person, and the only one named after the loser, at that. *That* was political correctness run amok.") Eventually Baker requested and received a transfer to another park. Ground has been broken for the Indian memorial, but construction remains stalled due to a lack of funds.

Disputes like these are not unique to the United States. South Africa must grapple with how to treat holidays, statues, and other public symbols that honor an Afrikaaner history of violence against and oppression of blacks. The Bosnian government has faced paralyzing disagreement over what should go on a flag, an official seal, and even license plates. Indian Muslims vigorously protested the changing of Bombay's name to Mumbai by a local government dominated by Hindu nationalists, interpreting the new name as a celebration of linguistic and religious chauvinism. In 1994 Australia endured riots and the firebombing of churches, community centers, and government buildings in a battle largely over what name the state would use to refer to Macedonians in the country. (The then-prime minister, trying to placate Greek Australians after his government extended diplomatic recognition to the Former Yugoslav Republic of Macedonia, adopted the phrase "Slav-Macedonians" and attempted to foist it on public institutions and broadcasters.) States adopt names for regions, cities, ethnic groups, and even themselves; they adopt flags and anthems; they commemorate the past through holidays, parks, proclamations, statues, and monuments. All of these symbolic state actions express an official viewpoint about the character of the state, its culture, and its history. Disputes over that character, over who is a member of the state, over how to interpret the way the state gained control over its current lands and people, over what is worth celebrating in the state's history, are all reflected in disputes over those symbols.

In none of these cases are any rights or resources, any property or powers, directly at stake. The state actions do not limit any person's liberty or seize any person's goods. As such, they seem to fall outside the scope of theories of justice, as those are usually understood. No one in particular is harmed by them in a way, for example, that would give standing for relief by a court in an Anglo-American judicial system. (There are exceptions—most conspicuously, US courts are willing to strike down the state adoption of some religious symbolism as violating the Establishment Clause of the First Amendment. But ordinarily, state symbols may not be challenged in court.)

Political matters may fall outside the scope of justice, however, and still be within the scope of a broader political morality. Some state symbols are morally preferable to others; some official speech is morally wrong. Standards for judgment are difficult to come by, though, especially in a political culture (like America's) accustomed to translating all serious moral disputes about politics into the language of rights-violations and constitutionality.

In his comparative study of ethnic conflict, political scientist Donald Horowitz finds that "symbolic claims are not readily amenable to compromise. In this, they differ from claims deriving wholly from material interest. Whereas material advancement can be measured both relatively and absolutely, the status advancement of one ethnic group is entirely relative to the status of others." Not only are disputes over state symbols often zero-sum; they are sometimes all-or-nothing. With so little room for compromise, there is often little incentive for moderation.

Ethnic conflicts are not always or primarily about symbolism, even when words and symbols are part of what's at stake. Flags and coats of arms often count for much less than concrete matters: Who has the right to use which language when? Who controls which land? Which cultural traditions will be banned, which ones tolerated? Will constitutional arrangements allow for any self-government by minorities? Members of minority cultures and ethnic groups are imprisoned for speaking their native languages, dispossessed of their lands, expelled and made into refugees, and sometimes enslaved, raped, or slaughtered. Nor are these high stakes limited to obviously-explosive places like the Balkans or the African Great Lakes; there are live questions of justice from indigenous land rights to the toleration of minority religious practices in most Western liberal democracies. Some academics say that questions of recognition and respect, not questions of rights and resources, are at the heart of ethnic politics; but this thought seems to me a luxury of immersion in educational institutions, which have more direct control over curricula, mottoes, and holidays than over legal liberties and powers.

But still, such concrete questions of rights and resources do not make up the whole of ethnic and cultural politics. Issues of identity and recognition, symbolic issues, play an important part as well; and there is no general tendency for symbolic disputes to be less intense, to be taken less seriously by the participants. Liberalism is right to give rights and resources moral priority over recognition and symbols; but that should not prevent liberals from seeing the tremendous importance symbolic disputes can have to their participants. Liberalism, and a liberal state, ought to come to grips with the moral importance of symbolism.

Responses to Symbolism

We should not, however, detach our moral understanding of state symbolism from our moral understanding of concrete injustices committed against subordinated ethnic groups. The participants in disputes over state symbols are often all too aware of the close relationship between the two. State symbols often celebrate and commemorate a history of cruelty, injustice, and exclusion. They often aim—or obviously invite the charge that they aim—at symbolically excluding a minority from full membership in the polity. They suggest that the polity's past wrongs against a group are precisely what makes the polity worthy of celebration and loyalty.

What's worse, they make this suggestion in the voice of the citizenry, including members of the wronged group. When the state speaks (that is, when state officials adopt a flag, name a place or a group, write the text on a statue or the educational materials for a national park, and so on) it claims to do more than just offer an opinion into the marketplace of ideas. It claims to speak on behalf of all its members. Hobbes long ago noticed that built into the idea of authorization, and therefore the idea of authority, was the claim that the citizens "authored" the state's actions. The idea has even more resonance when the authority's actions consist of words. Democratic states, especially, claim that their words and actions in some sense issue from the people as a whole. Whether and to what degree these claims are justified are questions that may be set aside for present purposes. But the fact that they are made (and widely believed) makes certain state speech particularly objectionable. Sometimes state speech or symbols that glorify (for example) past state violence seems like an implicit threat to unleash the violence again. But even without that component, citizens ought not to be insulted or degraded by an agency that professes to represent them and to speak in their name.

Although many disputes over ethnic and cultural symbolism are strictly zero-sum, not all of them are. Symbolic status is not *entirely* relative to the status of others. Suppose one's culture is routinely degraded and humiliated, pronounced to be primitive and bestial. Then policy changes, and members of that particular culture are now considered to be human. A gain in status may impose a corresponding status loss for others, since the other group's sense of its own *superiority* may be diminished. But commonly the previously superior group is not degraded in turn. One group's liberation from humiliation does not require another group's humiliation. Now, none of this is true about the symbolism of national character. A state becomes officially binational only at the expense of its being national. Malays or Fijians gain symbolic priority only at the expense of Chinese-Malaysians or Indian-Fijians. But minimal symbolic recognition need not be zero-sum in quite the same way.

Advocates of a strong form of what philosopher Charles Taylor has called "the politics of recognition" suggest that public invisibility is also a kind of symbolic exclusion and degradation. When there are no public monuments that commemorate an ethnic group's history, when no official holidays are established in honor of any member of a given minority, when public buildings are all named for members of the culturally dominant group, then, too, the state has humiliated some of its citizens and has committed a moral wrong.

This line of argument is sometimes justified, but it is a hazardous one. It invites a kind of political pandering and one-upsmanship ("Anything less than proportionality, or even parity, in official holidays constitutes invisibility!").

Much official symbolism is inevitably part of a spoils system, handed out in an attempt to appeal to a particular constituency or interest group. In the United States, perhaps the purest example of this kind of pork-barrel symbolism is the unending stream of official commemorative days, weeks, and months announced by Congress and other levels of government. Most people never know when National Goat Cheese Week or National Veterans of the Grenada Conflict Day come to pass; they are noted only in the Congressional Record and in lobbying-group newsletters. They provide an absurdly faint shadow of public recognition, since the public never knows they exist; the state speaks a word of praise to the constituency group, but no one else ever hears it. Yet lobbying groups continue to insist on these faux-commemorations, and Congress and state and local governments continue to devote time and resources to discussing and establishing them.

Insisting on quotas for public symbolism threatens to reduce all symbolism to that level; it diminishes whatever value public symbolism might have. Indeed it is self-defeating. The affirmation and recognition that public commemoration confers is dependent on the lingering thought that the commemoration is provided for some public reason and not for the purpose of providing affirmation. When that thought ceases to linger, as it long since has in the case of the pointless official days and weeks, no real recognition is provided. As morally different as public and private speech sometimes are, there is an important similarity. The coin of public honor can be debased, just like the coin of praise from a person who lavishes the same compliments on all (or from the person whose kind words for the intelligence or charm of others are uncorrelated with their intelligence or charm but highly correlated with their wealth, or their social standing, or their ethnicity).

A strong politics of recognition might also endorse a rule that simply allows each group to define its own labels and symbols. Outsiders, and the state, should accept each group's claims about its own name, symbols, and so on. While this may answer the question of "who decides?" across a certain range of cases, it does not dampen the conflicts over the decisions. It is just not the case that what one group calls itself is of no concern to another. The crux of the conflict between Greeks and Macedonians (in Australia as in the Balkans) was that two groups were both laying claim to the word "Macedonian," with Greece maintaining that "Macedonian" described only a subset of "Greek." What if white Protestant Americans tried to reserve for themselves the label "American," or the name "God's people?" I do not suggest that either move is likely; but the possibility illustrates that one group's preferred name can easily be an insult to another. A liberal state cannot prevent persons from referring to themselves however they like; but it cannot simply adopt their preferred terms for its own usage. Moreover, cultural groups are too heterogeneous for us to assume that the name chosen by leaders or a majority will not be experienced as an insult by other members of the community.

Words Can Never Hurt Me?

Children are taught to say, "Words can never hurt me." Since symbolism does not affect any rights or resources of any person, some think that there can be nothing morally important to say about it, nothing worth disputing. Words, expressions, and symbols are not the stuff of justice or morality, or even of morally interesting politics. They are "only words." What statues are erected and what holidays are celebrated are inevitably arbitrary, but they fail to meet the threshold test of warranting moral praise or condemnation; they have no actual effect on individual persons. The justification would vary a bit, but this basic position might be embraced by anyone from a conservative opposed to "political correctness" to an Old Left socialist who finds symbolic disputes to be distractions from the serious business of economic politics.

To indicate what this position leaves out, consider this example: What if the United States Census Bureau adopted a racial epithet as its name for one of the racial categories into which it divides Americans? Even the vicious epithet used for so long against African Americans is, after all, only a word. But it is a word that is tied up with a long history of violence, public and private. It is a word that is understood, by whites and blacks alike, to exclude blacks not just from full citizenship but from full humanity. Its use by a speaker with power or authority is nearly a threat. Leaving aside questions like whether it would be a rights violation or whether it would be legally justiciable, what reason could we possibly have for declining to say that it would be wrong for the state to adopt this epithet for common use? When we recall that the state professes to speak in the name of its citizens, "words can never hurt me" becomes an even more obviously insufficient response to such cases. One need not accept any claims about language constructing social reality or language forming the basis of oppression in order to think that *this speech would be wrong*. In the name of all of the citizenry, it would denigrate and (symbolically but painfully) attack a significant portion. In an allegedly authoritative voice, it would state that the history of injustice of which the word reminds blacks and whites alike was acceptable, even commendable.

"Words can never hurt me" has a bit too proud a place as an argument in American political culture. Sometimes civil libertarians suggest that words and expressions are immune from political and moral criticism in order to defuse the threat of censorship. Condemning another's speech is too quickly interpreted as a prelude to a violation of freedom of speech, and so supporters of freedom of speech sometimes retreat into moral relativism when faced with reprehensible forms of expression. Of course, *some* criticism of others' words does plausibly contain an implicit threat of censorship (for instance, Congressional hearings or resolutions about classes of private speech and expression—such as music lyrics). But citizens' moral criticism of state speech does not. It offers no threat of coercion, no threat to the diversity of expressed ideas, no threat to individuality, no threat to the democratic process.

Some liberals maintain that the state should not publicly endorse particular points of view, particular cultural identities, particular visions of the good life.

"Content neutrality" is a concept from the American constitutional jurisprudence of speech regulation, but might be elevated to a general liberal principle of state action and speech. Content neutrality, however, is a principle for evaluating an actor who referees speakers, not a principle for evaluating speech itself. No particular speech, expression, or symbol can be content neutral, so if the principle of content neutrality is applicable to state speech, that means the state may not speak. Liberal neutrality could be supposed to require that the state avoid official symbolism, which necessarily elevates some substantive claims about cultural communities and their worth over others.

The seemingly interminable disputes in the post-Dayton Bosnian state about national symbols—a flag, a coat of arms, a national anthem, even license plates—illustrate the appeal of this approach. Symbols which are Muslim, Serbian, avowedly multiethnic, or avowedly nonethnic are all unacceptable to some constituents and political leaders. None of the symbols are neutral. Both liberal neutrality and prudence might counsel abandoning the project of adopting *any* symbols of state. A long history of mutual abuses might leave little room for acceptable public commemoration. Fights over symbolism in any event have little incentive for moderation or compromise, and sometimes any choice of symbol seems designed to provoke some part of the population. Modern states are in the habit of having anthems, coats of arms, and the rest, but little is lost if they are sometimes forgone. I doubt that the principle of liberal neutrality ought to be extended so as to insist upon strict neutrality in all state speech and, therefore, forbid state speech. But prudence and a careful attention to avoiding provocation will sometimes counsel silence rather than a fight over what shall be said, what symbol chosen.

In the United States, official language laws with much bite have been held to violate the First Amendment. Most remaining official English proposals seek largely symbolic declarations. We cannot pretend that the state is linguistically neutral; English is and will remain the *de facto* language of state. But there seems little need for the symbolism of an official declaration, little reason for the state officially to endorse English. State silence would be better.

We are left with a standard that treats symbolic celebrations of past instances of ethnic violence, cruelty, and injustice as worthy of moral condemnation, while leaving most other cases of symbolism to the considerations of prudence. If a state cannot affirm each group on its own terms, it can at least refrain from celebrating wrongs against any of them. Humiliation is a debatable standard but must not be simply a subjective one; we (whoever we are evaluating a particular cultural dispute) must ask whether the person or people are right to feel humiliated. State symbols that celebrate a history of violence and cruelty against a particular group—say, the Confederate battle flag—are legitimately taken to be humiliating. So are the preambular statements in some states' constitutions that the state belongs to a particular ethnic group; the words may not strip anyone of citizenship, but they symbolically exclude from citizenship.

The Symbols of Slavery

The debates and disputes over the symbolic legacy of slavery in the United States are widespread and can be bitter. There has been considerable agitation for an official apology for slavery from the US government. New Orleans has adopted a rule that public schools should not be named for slaveowners; this attracted international attention when a school named for George Washington was renamed. During the battle to integrate the public schools, some southern states resurrected the battle flag of the Confederate States of America as a symbol of their defiance; it flies over some state capitols to this day. Statues of Confederate leaders and monuments to the Confederate war dead dot the South. A statue of Queen Catherine of Braganza, which is supposed to stand overlooking New York's borough of Queens which was named for her, has been the subject of bitter controversy because some activists have charged her with profiting from the slave trade. This is false; indeed, Catherine left money in her will to be used to free slaves. She was linked to the slave trade only insofar as the two states of which she was royalty, Portugal and the United Kingdom, were at that time involved in it. Nonetheless, the dispute has gone on for years and continues to prevent the statue's placement.

The passage of time matters in symbolic disputes. Retaining the month names of July and August does not at all connote official approval of the millennia-old wrongs committed by the Caesars, and no one (not republicans, not Jews or Christians, not the descendants of the Gauls) can reasonably claim to be humiliated or symbolically excluded from the polity because of it. Slavery was abolished a century and a third ago. However, American blacks did not attain full legal equality for a century after that. Violence against blacks was pervasive in the South for decades after slavery was abolished. And the upsurge in official Confederate symbolism after *Brown vs. Board* confirms and cements the link between those symbols and their unjust history.

This history does not mean that every symbol at which some African Americans take offense really is a humiliating endorsement of past injustice. There is a difference between celebrating figures for the war they fought to defend slavery (Robert E. Lee, Jefferson Davis) and celebrating figures who owned slaves but who are being celebrated for other reasons (George Washington). Similarly, the dispute over

Queen Catherine shows that we should not simply defer to every activist who invokes a history of injustice. Once the facts become known, a statue of Catherine cannot rightly be interpreted as a celebration of slavery or of the slave trade.

On the other hand, the emphasis on slavery, and on not symbolically endorsing it, is justified. Even if the answers given in particular cases are wrong, the questions (does this state action symbolically celebrate or glorify a history of shameful wrongs?) are the right ones to ask. Avoiding such institutional humiliation and official endorsement of past cruelty no doubt seems like a minimal standard, compared with a full-blooded politics of recognition. But it is a minimal standard that would demand quite widespread changes in official symbolism, not least in the United States itself.

This chapter appeared previously in the *Report from the Institute for Philosophy & Public Policy*, vol. 20, no. 4 (Fall 2002). Some of the themes of this present essay are discussed further in Jacob T. Levy, *The Multiculturalism of Fear* (Oxford University Press, 2000).

Sources

Mike Tobin, "Indian Memorial Renews Battle at Little Bighorn," *Times Picayune* (August 25, 1996); Donald Horowitz, *Ethnic Groups in Conflict* (University of California Press, 1986). For an examination of related legal problems, and more generally for an exploration of the present issues that focus on commemorations of the Confederacy, see Sanford Levinson, *Written in Stone: Public Monuments in Changing Societies* (Duke University Press, 1998).

Lessons from the Brooklyn Museum Controversy

Peter Levine

How many art exhibitions are accompanied by a "Health Warning"? Visitors to the Brooklyn Museum's 1999 "Sensation" show were told: "The contents of this exhibition may cause shock, vomiting, confusion, panic, euphoria, and anxiety. If you suffer from high blood pressure, a nervous disorder, or palpitations, you should consult your doctor before viewing this exhibition."

Those brave (and hip) enough to enter were exposed to paintings, sculptures, videos, and installations by a group called The Young British Artists. The works that had the best chance of causing shock and vomiting included Marcus Harvey's portrait of the child-killer Myra Hindley, painted with real children's handprints; Damien Hirst's "A Thousand Years," composed of a decaying cow's head with live flies and maggots; and Chris Ofili's "Holy Virgin Mary," which incorporates elephant dung and photographs of genitalia.

As the predictable uproar about the exhibition erupted, New York Mayor Rudolph Giuliani tried to slash the museum's funding. He claimed that the decision not to admit unaccompanied children to "Sensation" put the museum in violation of its city lease and subjected it to eviction. He also argued that the government may not finance blasphemous art, because to do so breaches the separation of church and state.

These arguments were rejected in federal court; the city was compelled to refund the money it had withheld. The mayor did score

47

points, however, by alleging (with some plausibility) that "Sensation" was a "scam": a conspiracy involving Christie's auction house, the Brooklyn Museum, and the owner of the art, Charles Saatchi, to raise the market value of his collection. Meanwhile, the mayor's opponents accused him of using a cultural controversy to score points with conservative voters as he prepared to compete with Hillary Clinton for New York's open Senate seat.

Behind all the ritualistic name-calling and litigation was a serious issue: the relationship between art and democracy. This relationship has been troubled and unproductive for several decades. I think that politicians and artists must share the blame.

Imagine that we were debating welfare reform or zoning instead of elephant dung on "The Holy Virgin Mary." In these more ordinary cases, we would want elected officials to supervise decisions that involved public money, but we would expect them to act only after reasonable public deliberation. We would ask everyone involved to heed multiple perspectives, respect facts, achieve as much common ground as possible, and examine arguments rather than assault their opponents' characters.

This is the deliberative approach to democratic politics. I will argue that artists and politicians ought to behave more deliberatively than they have in their recent skirmishes. But deliberation is only relevant if arts policy belongs within the normal give-and-take of politics. Both sides in the Brooklyn Museum controversy claimed—in contrast—that a high constitutional principle settled the question of arts funding. If they were right, then neither the public nor elected officials had any business deliberating about particular works of art or about arts policy in general.

Charges of "Censorship"

One group, civil libertarians, detected unconstitutional censorship in New York City's treatment of the Brooklyn Museum. According to the American Civil Liberties Union, the museum was an institution "devoted to discourse and expression." Once the government had decided to fund such an institution, it could not use its money to influence decisions about what images were exhibited. According to the ACLU:

> Just as academic judgments are left to the academics, curatorial judgments must be left to the curators. Just as a state cannot use its fund-

ing authority to micro-manage the content of a professor's lectures, the First Amendment also bars Mayor Giuliani from using City funding to dictate the content of a curated art exhibition.

In its brief, the ACLU explicitly charged the mayor with censorship. Some people have gone further and seen a reduction in the overall level of government support for the arts as "a de facto form of censorship."

US District Judge Nina Gershon resolved the case in the museum's favor but on narrower grounds, concluding that:

> The issue is not whether the City could have been required to provide funding for the Sensations exhibit, but whether the Museum, having been allocated a general operating subsidy, can now be penalized with the loss of that subsidy, and ejectment from a City-owned building, because of the perceived viewpoint of the works in that exhibit. The answer to that question is no.

With this ruling, civil libertarians won a battle in the war over arts policy. But the Constitution cannot compel governments to subsidize art in the first place. When the Supreme Court ruled in 1998 that individual artists may not be denied federal grants because of the content of their work, Congress simply canceled all support for individual artists. If democratic leaders are given the choice either to fund everything that curators call "art," or to support no exhibitions at all, many will choose the latter option. In New York City, museums are powerful and will probably continue to receive tax money no matter what the mayor thinks. (However, some observers fear that he will punish the particular institutions that sued him.) In other communities where the arts have far less political clout, complete denial of funding is a likely response to adverse court rulings.

I am not arguing that courts should never strike down state arts policies that violate the First Amendment. For example, the City of New York probably acted unconstitutionally when it made an unrestricted grant to a museum and then withdrew the money *ex post facto* because of the content of the exhibited art. How *much* flexibility the government enjoys under the First Amendment is a matter of ongoing legal controversy. But regardless of the proper answer to this question, broader issues remain that will never be settled in court, because only the public has the right to decide them. Do the arts need and deserve public subsidies? If so, what are the best priorities for our arts budget? For instance, should more money go to museums, schools, or artists? Should the public fund amateurs, students, or professionals? Should we subsidize big-city artists, or regional institutions? Should we exhibit contemporary works, or Old Masters? Should our arts budget promote video installations, or novels, or public monuments?

These matters should not and will not be settled by judges. Before the larger jury of public opinion, the avant-garde may have a difficult case to make, but it cannot hide behind charges of "censorship." Arts programs and subsidies are never entirely different from appropriations for schools or homeless shelters; inevitably, they are matters to be settled by some combination of majority rule, horse trading, delegation to professional experts, and (if we're lucky) constructive public deliberation.

Sinful and Tyrannical Subsidies?

In court, Mayor Giuliani argued just the reverse of the civil libertarian position. Whereas the museum's lawyers wanted to prevent elected officials from refusing to fund controversial art under almost any circumstances, the mayor claimed that the state may never support such expression. It is always wrong, he said, to use public money to finance "vicious attacks on religion."

But if the state must be neutral about matters of faith, then it cannot discriminate against irreligious expression. (This has been the Supreme Court's view since a 1952 case, *Joseph Burstyn, Inc. v. Wilson*.) Perhaps the mayor's real position was that public funds should never support anything that causes very deep offense to some. "If you are a government subsidized enterprise," he said, "then you can't do things that desecrate the most deeply held and personal views of the people in society." In the preamble to the *Virginia Bill for Establishing Religious Freedom,* Thomas Jefferson wrote, "to compel a man to furnish contributions of money for the propagation of opinions which he disbelieves and abhors, is sinful and tyrannical."

Although this "Jeffersonian Principle" is not explicit in the US Constitution, it is often invoked in First Amendment cases. For example, some people argue that it precludes unions from lobbying the government with their members' dues, student governments from using mandatory activity fees for controversial purposes, and Congress from funding political campaigns with tax money.

The Jeffersonian Principle has something going for it. The fact that some citizens "abhor" the Confederate flag seems a sufficient reason not to fly it over a statehouse, because doing so expresses official disrespect for their views. However, if we apply the Jeffersonian Principle literally and comprehensively, there can be no democracy. As the Supreme Court noted in 1984, "virtually every congressional appropriation will to some extent involve a use of public money . . . to which some taxpayers may object." This applies to state acts of *expression* as well as to other governmental activities.

For instance, the secretary of state's latest pronouncements on Africa may enrage me, yet I have helped to pay her salary. Every day, public school teachers propound before tender ears ideas that would make some of us cringe. For that matter, think of the portraits in City Hall's Blue Room, where the mayor meets the press. They show an array of dead white males, including Jefferson (who owned slaves) and Edward Livingston (who served as an antebellum Louisiana senator after leaving New York in a hurry). I happen to think that Jefferson's portrait is a worthy symbol, but not everyone would agree. As Hugh Field, a freshman at Pratt Institute, told the *New York Times,* "I find the mayor offensive, but that doesn't mean I'm going to stop paying my taxes."

It seems to me that citizens and elected officials ought to pay some attention to the Jeffersonian Principle and try to avoid decisions that will offend people's deepest convictions. But sometimes offense should be given—either because those who take umbrage are morally wrong, or because discord is the price we must pay for having a robust, diverse, and equitable public debate. Mayor Giuliani claimed that the offense taken by some Catholics automatically made "Sensation" an inappropriate use of tax money. He thereby sought to end (or circumvent) the public debate about the particular works exhibited at the Brooklyn Museum—just as civil libertarians hoped to evade the debate by charging "censorship" in federal court.

A More Constructive Approach

Let's assume, instead, that democratic institutions may and will decide whether to fund art. It would be useful for the public and elected leaders to deliberate, rather than leave the results to brute majority rule or logrolling. In deliberation, a wide range of relevant considerations can be aired, stereotypes and hasty judgments can be debunked, and satisfactory compromises can be devised. In debates about arts policy, deliberation has a further advantage. Whether the state chooses to fund controversial art or to shun it, some are offended by what the government seems to be expressing on their behalf and with their money. It is a consolation to be able to articulate the contrary view during a public debate.

In *Democracy and Disagreement,* Amy Gutmann and Dennis Thompson set high (and perhaps unrealistic) standards for "deliberation." Every argument must appeal to reasons or principles that could be accepted by other people who are also deliberating. Every empirical claim must be testable by reliable, non-private methods. All reasons and arguments must be offered in public. All participants (including ordinary citizens) owe explanations to everyone else whom their decisions may affect. As they deliberate, they are supposed to be open-minded, to acknowledge that their opponents' positions are also motivated by moral beliefs, and to explain their views in terms that minimize their disapproval of others.

By the Gutmann-and-Thompson standard, the public debate about "Sensation" was not deliberative. Many in the Art World (a loose network of established artists, agents, curators, critics, and patrons) attacked Mayor Giuliani's allegedly selfish motivations. But even if his only goal was to gain votes, his position could still be correct, his judgment sound. The lowest personal insult was delivered by Glenn Scott Wright, Chris Ofili's London agent. Wright told the *Washington Post* that Mayor Giuliani's behavior "is both totalitarian and fascist, a reprisal of the Nazi regime's censorship." This kind of remark makes a decaying cow's head look like a subtle and perceptive statement.

A half dozen editorials implied that it was a mistake for the public to deliberate about whether to support contemporary art. Even the most offensive works might later turn out to be great—weren't Shakespeare and Joyce controversial in their times? According to these observers, the public was not entitled to make the critical judgment that some work is bad.

The controversial art itself had an in-your-face, shock-the-bourgeoisie attitude; it was not calculated to persuade people on the other side of a cultural debate. Ofili told the *New York Times:* "I don't feel as though I have to defend [my work]. You never know what's going to offend people, and I don't feel it's my place to say any more." Maybe it's not a painter's job to justify his art in words. But if the Brooklyn curators had expected their show to provoke careful thought and dialogue, then they wouldn't have boasted that the "contents of this exhibition may cause shock, vomiting, confusion." Still, the art in

"Sensation" can be defended. The *New York Times* critic Michael Kimmelman praised Ofili's "lightness of spirit." In the *Nation*, Arthur Danto argued that the elephant dung on the Virgin couldn't be derogatory, because Ofili (who was born in Nigeria) used the same material in Afrobluff, an image of African slaves. This is the kind of relevant fact that surfaces when people deliberate.

Indeed, Danto's review of "Sensation" was packed with arguments that could persuade open-minded readers to support the show. For instance, against those who claim that any fool can submerge a shark in formaldehyde, Danto insisted:

> But *imagining* doing it requires a degree of artistic intuition of a very rare order, since one would have to anticipate what it would look like and what effect it would have on the viewer. The work in fact has the power, sobriety and majesty of a cathedral, some of which, of course, must be credited to the shark itself.

Deliberation and the Avant-Garde

Danto's review exemplifies deliberation; but how deliberative must critics, artists, curators, patrons, and agents be? All of Gutmann and Thompson's examples involve matters that public officials debate: laws, appropriations, court rulings, and administrative decisions. It seems philistine and misguided to ask artists and their interpreters to become policy analysts. Nevertheless, I believe that avant-garde artists can and should pay more attention to deliberative values than they do.

Consider an example of politically motivated or *engagé* art that fails as rhetoric because the artist does not know how to persuade average Americans who disagree with him. On the wall of the Whitney Museum, Hans Haacke has printed Mayor Giuliani's remarks about the "Sensation" show in *Fraktur*, Hitler's preferred script. The sound of marching boots emerges from nearby trash cans, while newspaper clippings and the text of the First Amendment lie on the floor, apparently ready to be trampled.

This installation, entitled "Sanitation," criticizes a public policy (the revocation of the Brooklyn Museum's funding). It offers reasons for its conclusion and may promote serious thinking—although perhaps not exactly the thoughts that Haacke had intended. On these grounds, "Sanitation" qualifies as an exercise in deliberation, but it is an extremely clumsy example. It invites the response that its artist has

trivialized the Holocaust and misunderstood the present political situation. Rudy Giuliani is no Adolf Hitler; besides, the mayor's office
lacks dictatorial powers. Perhaps Haacke feels that he dwells among
the complacent subjects of a police state, so he must issue shocking
statements in order to provoke dialogue and resistance. However, this
view is false. The fact that "Sanitation" poses as "art" is no excuse for
its bad arguments and *ad hominem* attacks.

Unlike Haacke's "Sanitation," the works in "Sensation" do not
directly engage policy questions. Often they challenge the traditional
limits of art by combining a cool, museum-style presentation with
appalling materials, such as human blood. But even these works can be
germane to policy decisions. The public (and public officials) must consider the definitions, purposes, and limits of "art" whenever the question of cultural subsidies arises. If postmodern artists successfully
undermine the distinction between art and despised objects such as
cows' heads, then the case for arts subsidies will weaken. More generally, shocking the bourgeoisie is no way to persuade them to pay for art.
Representative Brian Bilbray is a moderate California Republican who
votes to fund the National Endowment for the Arts. "You can't expect
public funds to be used on the cutting edge," he told the *San Diego
Union-Tribune*, "because artists have to be responsible to the people
who pay the bills, just like Michelangelo had to answer to the pope."

Another class of works in "Sensation" invites us to change our
ways of observing other people, perhaps for moral reasons. For
instance, Danto argues that Jenny Saville's cropped painting of a
naked woman with contour lines like those in a topographical map
("Trace") challenges our tendency to objectify the female body. Saville
is heir to a long tradition of artists who seek to shock us out of our
visual habits and assumptions. Consider a famously controversial
American work, Andres Serrano's photograph of an old woman with
withered breasts about to perform oral sex on a young man ("The
Kiss," 1996). The purpose of this image is surely to make men question their desire for images of nubile female bodies.

In principle, such works could change social norms for the better,
with implications for public policy. But it is unlikely that many men
who happily employ the "male gaze" when they look at real women
are going to view images by Saville and Serrano. Except when there is
a controversy about public money, the Art World mostly talks to itself.
Avant-garde artists could once command a large audience merely by
crossing boundaries of taste and propriety, but now the public is not

so easily shocked, and only pop culture frequently achieves *succès de scandale*. The *Daily News*'s Michael Daly wrote: "As viewed in the catalogue, 'Sensation' is now about as sensational as Beanie Babies." Ofili's "Holy Virgin Mary" still managed to attract headlines by appalling the Catholic Church, but the only people who seemed to notice Jenny Saville's paintings were respectful art critics who already opposed sexism and the male gaze.

Therefore, instead of trying to astound the bourgeoisie, *engagé* artists might employ more deliberative techniques. It need not be burdensome to have to persuade average citizens by using reasons that they can share and by listening carefully to their responses. These are democratic skills that can inspire the fine arts, as the long tradition of American public art testifies. One high point was the New Deal, when artists employed by the Works Progress (later Projects) Administration's Federal Art Project (WPA/FAP) generated hundreds of thousands of murals, posters, and statues in consultation with "co-operating sponsors"—usually local governments. Even today, Christo saves all the correspondence, plans, environmental-impact statements, and petitions that he needs before he gets permission to "wrap" a building. These objects (which are often beautiful) become part of the art; they celebrate his respectful engagement with democratic communities.

To engage the public in dialogue does not require behaving in the civil, courteous, and reasonable fashion that we would prefer in the US Senate or the Supreme Court. When the circumstances demand it, the artist and philosopher Adrian Piper distributes small cards with the following text: "Dear Friend. I am black. I am sure you did not realize this when you made/laughed at/agreed with that racist remark." This is effective political performance art. It challenges not only the recipient but also Piper's whole audience to examine their consciences in ways that could change social norms and ultimately affect public policy decisions. Perhaps Piper's cards do not exemplify "deliberation," as Gutmann and Thompson define it. For example, when she appears to acknowledge the good faith of others ("Dear Friend, I'm sure you did not realize . . ."), she may be bitingly sarcastic rather than sincere. But an artist can contribute to an important democratic conversation even if her rhetoric is not itself civil.

The Politics of Art

More so than artists, elected officials and political commentators have a duty both to deliberate and to foster reasonable public discussion. To be sure, politicians sometimes face a dilemma. If they behave civilly and thoughtfully, they may lose elections to opponents who hold what they consider pernicious views and methods. The competitive nature of politics excuses some lapses from the Gutmann-and-Thompson norms. But that does not mean that everything that powerful politicians say is acceptable from the public's point of view. Similarly, newspapers must sell copies in a competitive marketplace. But they do not have to discard civility and reasonableness in order to capture market share.

During the "Sensation" debate, New York City looked for technical excuses to penalize the museum, rather than advance a cogent critique of the art. (I leave aside the conflict-of-interest allegation, which raised important but complex questions about museum practices generally.) The mayor never addressed the arguments that Danto and others made in defense of the Young British Artists; indeed, he never attended the show.

Meanwhile, in the *New York Post*, columnist Rod Dreher called the exhibition's organizers "Prospect Park Poo Peddlers" and accused them of "intellectual mountebankery and self-righteous leftie mewling." This was extreme, but more respectable voices repeatedly accused Ofili of being an anti-Catholic bigot, even though the artist denied the charge and explained that his use of elephant dung symbolized "regeneration." Mike Barnicle of the *New York Daily News* presented a particularly caustic analogy:

> Ofili, himself a Catholic, is black as night. Imagine for a moment if a guy named Kelly sat down at an easel, produced a painting of a black man being dragged behind a pickup truck driven by a laughing rabbi with a smiling Billy Graham standing on the bumper, urinating on the victim's battered corpse and decided to call it art.

Liberal museum goers, Barnicle concluded, would be the first to demand that "Kelly's" work be banned. But it's hard to see how the wicked and cartoonish painting in Barnicle's story could resemble "The Blessed Virgin Mary."

The mayor denounced any and all art that (as a factual matter) offends some citizens. Instead, he could have explained why the particular works in dispute were not worth exhibiting and then listened to any serious replies. At the same time, he could have considered his own authority to evaluate works of art. As a general rule, should elected officials intervene in specific decisions by museums, or should they give curators (or public administrators, or independent experts, or committees of artists) a free hand to decide what works to exhibit? Under what circumstances is political intervention appropriate? A well-organized debate about arts funding would open with such procedural questions.

One of the worst effects of the "wars" over arts funding is that we have not been able to deliberate about such issues as a public or in Congress. We might also ask: Is the occasional scandal a necessary price to pay for subsidizing art that is mostly innocuous? Can we avoid such scandals through skilful vetting procedures? Or should we actually be happiest when tax money pays for unpopular ideas, thereby broadening the debate? In general, is state support for the arts necessary, or would the private sector finance art adequately? Would a different system for paying artists produce better or worse works? What kind of art do we need, anyway?

In this discussion, it is worth considering the WPA example, which shows that state support can encourage artists to begin constructive dialogues with the broad public without sacrificing their independence. In contrast, the Young British Artists got their start in the late 1980s, when state funding was at its low ebb in Britain. They began making scandalous artistic "statements" partly in order to attract attention and sales, since there were few grants to be had. All the works in "Sensation" are now owned by Margaret Thatcher's former advertising guru, an entrepreneur who has made considerable profit in the art business. In this case, at least, the market rewarded scandal. The best way to encourage more responsible art may be to subsidize it publicly, but that's not going to happen if elected leaders feel they must second-guess every curator's decision.

It seems to me that if you dislike the values that are reflected in contemporary art, then you should make overtures to artists, not just threaten to cut off their financing. For their part, artists who dislike conventional beliefs and values need ways to communicate with average Americans, not just other members of the Art World. But the encounter between politics and art is not likely to be illuminating until we have a different kind of political leadership—and a different avant-garde.

This chapter appeared previously in *Report from the Institute for Philosophy & Public Policy*, vol. 20, no. 2/3 (Summer 2000).

Sources

Brooklyn Museum of Art web site at www.brooklynart.org (visited in September 1999); David M. Herszenhorn, "Brooklyn Museum Accused of Trying to Lift Art Value," *New York Times* (September 30, 1999); *Brooklyn Institute of Arts & Sciences v. Giuliani, Memorandum of Law Submitted on Behalf of the New York Civil Liberties Union, et al. as amicus curiae*, 64 F. Supp. 2d 184 (1999); Tim Miller paraphrased in Joe Williams, "Performance Artist Miller Just Can't Stop Acting Up," *St. Louis Post-Dispatch* (November 20, 1998); *The Brooklyn Institute of Arts and Sciences v. The City of New York*, 64 F. Supp. 2d 184 (1999); David M. Herszenhorn, "With Art Battle in Spotlight, Mayor Revels in the Glare," *New York Times* (October 4, 1999); Dan Barry and Carol Vogel, "Giuliani Vows To Cut Subsidy Over 'Sick' Art," *New York Times* (September 23, 1999); Thomas Jefferson, preamble to A Bill for Establishing Religious Freedom, reproduced in Julian P. Boyd, ed., *The Papers of Thomas Jefferson* (Princeton, 1950); *Federal Communications Commission v. League of Women Voters of California*, 468 U.S. 364 (1984); David M. Herszenhorn, "Giuliani's Threats to Museum Make Exhibit a Hot Topic," *The New York Times* (September 27, 1999); Amy Gutmann and Dennis Thompson, *Democracy and Disagreement* (Harvard, 1996); Terry Teachout, "That Empty, Queasy 'Sensation'; Brooklyn Show Isn't Worth Such a Fuss," *Washington Post* (October 2, 1999); Carol Vogel, "Holding Fast to His Inspiration," *New York Times* (September 28, 1999); Michael Kimmelman, "After All That Yelling, Time to Think," *New York Times* (October 1, 1999); Arthur C. Danto, "'Sensation' in Brooklyn," *Nation* (November 1, 1999); Welton Jones, "Pro-NEA Bilbray Got What He Lobbied For," *The San Diego Union-Tribune* (July 28, 1998); Michael Daly, "Rudy's Making Real Sensation," *New York Daily News* (September 26, 1999) (www.nydailynews.com). Adrian Piper's business-card sized pieces are entitled "Angry Art" (self-published, 1985). To read the full text of Piper's "I am black . . ." card and for a discussion of the work in historical context, see www.vsw.org/afterimage/25year/cauley.html. Rod Dreher, "Leftist Loonies in Comedy of Manures," *New York Post* (September 30, 1999) (www.nypost.com); Mike Barnicle, "Museum's Dung Show Turns Us All into Losers," *New York Daily News* (October 3, 1999) (www.nydailynews.com).

Service in Deed?:
Civic Engagement and the
Prospect of Mandatory
Military Service

III

A Sketch of Some Arguments for Conscription

William A. Galston

In the run-up to the war against Iraq, an op-ed by congressional representative Charles Rangel (D-NY) rekindled a debate about the military draft; this was unexpected, because most scholars and an overwhelming majority of senior military leaders regarded this matter as settled. The Vietnam-era draft was regarded as arbitrary and unfair, and it was held responsible for dissension within the military as well as the wider society.

In the immediate wake of its disaster in Vietnam, the United States made an historic decision to end the draft and institute an All-Volunteer Force (AVF). On one level, it is hard to argue with success. The formula of high-quality volunteers combined with intensive training and investment in state-of-the-art equipment has produced by far the most formidable military in history. Evidence suggests that the military's performance, especially since 1990, has bolstered public trust and confidence. For example, a recent Gallup Poll of public opinion trends since the end of the Vietnam war in 1975 indicates that while the percentage of Americans expressing confidence in religious leaders fell from 68 to 45, and from 40 to 29 for Congress, the percentage expressing confidence in the military rose from under 30 to 78. Among eighteen- to twenty-nine-year olds, the confidence level rose from 20 to 64 percent. (Remarkably, these figures reflect sentiment in late 2002, *before* the impressive victory in Iraq.)

These gains in institutional performance and public confidence are impressive and significant, but they hardly end the discussion. As every reader of Machiavelli (or the Second Amendment) knows, the organization of the military is embedded in larger issues of citizenship and civic life. It is along these dimensions that the decision in favor of the AVF has entailed significant costs. First, the AVF reflects, and has contributed to the development of, what I call *optional citizenship*, the belief that being a citizen involves rights without responsibilities and that we need do for our country only what we choose to do. Numerous studies have documented the rise of individual choice as the dominant norm of contemporary American culture, and many young people today believe being a good person—decent, kind, caring, and tolerant—is all it takes to be a good citizen. This duty-free understanding of citizenship is comfortable and undemanding; it is also profoundly mistaken.

Second, the AVF contributes to what I call *spectatorial citizenship*—the premise that good citizens need not be active but can watch others doing the public's work on their behalf. This spectatorial outlook makes it possible to decouple the question of whether *we* as a nation should do X from the question of whether *I* would do or participate in X. In a discussion with his students during the Gulf War, philosophy professor Cheyney Ryan was struck by "how many of them saw no connection between whether the country should go to war and whether they would . . . be willing to fight in it." A similar disconnect exists today. Young adults have been more supportive of the war against Iraq than any other age group (with more than 70 percent in favor), but recent surveys have found an equal percentage would refuse to participate themselves.

As a counterweight to this decoupling, Ryan proposes what he calls the Principle of Personal Integrity: You should only endorse those military actions of your country in which you yourself would be willing to give your life. The difficulty is that integrity does not seem to require this kind of personal involvement in other public issues. For example, a citizen of integrity can favor a costly reform of the welfare system without being required to serve as a welfare caseworker. Presumably it is enough if citizens are willing to contribute their fair share of the program's expenses. So one might ask: Why is it not enough for citizens to contribute their fair share to maintain our expensive military establishment? Why should integrity require direct participation in the case of the military but not in other situations? This raises the question, to which I shall return, of when monetary contributions are morally acceptable substitutes for direct participation, and why.

Finally, the AVF has contributed to a widening gap between the orientation and experience of military personnel and that of the citizenry as a whole. To be sure, this is an empirically contested area, but some facts are not in dispute. First, since the inauguration of the AVF, the share of officers identifying themselves as Republican has nearly doubled, from 33 to 64 percent. (To be sure, officers were always technically volunteers, but as I can attest from personal experience, the threat of the draft significantly affected the willingness of young men to volunteer for officer candidacy.) Second, and more significantly, the share of elected officials with military experience has declined sharply. From 1900 through 1975, the percentage of members of Congress who were veterans was always higher than in the comparable age cohort of the general population. Since the mid-1990s, the congressional percentage has been lower, and it continues to fall.

Lack of military experience does not necessarily imply hostility to the military. Rather, it means ignorance of the nature of military service, as well as diminished capacity and confidence to assess critically the claims that military leaders make. (It is no accident that of all the postwar presidents, Dwight Eisenhower was clearly the most capable of saying no to the military's strategic assessments and requests for additional resources.)

For these reasons, among others, I believe that as part of a reconsideration of the relation between mandatory service and citizenship, we should review and revise the decision we made thirty years ago to institute an all-volunteer armed force. I hasten to add that I do not favor reinstituting anything like the Vietnam-era draft. It is hard to see how a reasonable person could prefer that fatally flawed system to today's arrangements. The question, rather, is whether feasible reforms could preserve the gains of the past thirty years while enlisting the military more effectively in the cause of civic renewal.

An Abuse of State Power?

My suggestion faces a threshold objection, however, to the effect that any significant shift back toward a mandatory system of military manpower would represent an abuse of state power. In a recent article, Judge Richard Posner drafts nineteenth-century political theorist John Stuart Mill as an ally in the cause of classical liberalism—a theory of limited government that provides an "unobtrusive framework for private activities." Limited government so conceived, Posner asserts, "has no ideology, no 'projects,' but is really just an association for mutual protection." Posner celebrates the recent emergence of what he calls the "Millian center"—a form of politics that (unlike the left) embraces economic liberty and (unlike the right) endorses personal liberty, and he deplores modern communitarianism's critique of untrammeled personal liberty in the name of the common good. High on Posner's bill of particulars is the recommendation of some (not all) communitarians to reinstitute a draft.

Mill misapplied. Before engaging Posner's own argument, I should note that his attempt to appropriate Mill's *On Liberty* to support an anti-conscription stance is deeply misguided. To clinch this point, I need only cite a few of the opening sentences from chapter 4, entitled "Of the Limits to the Authority of Society Over the Individual":

> [E]veryone who receives the protection of society owes a return for the benefit, and the fact of living in society renders it indispensable that each should be bound to observe a certain line of conduct toward the rest. This conduct consists, first, in not injuring the interests of one another, or rather certain interests which, either by express legal provision or by tacit understanding, ought to be considered as rights; *and secondly, in each person's bearing his share (to be fixed on some equitable principle) or the labors and sacrifices incurred for defending the society or its members from injury and molestation. These conditions society is justified in enforcing at all costs to those who endeavor to withhold fulfillment.*

Posner's view of Mill would make sense only if Mill had never written the words I have italicized.

The fair share argument. It is not difficult to recast Mill's position in the vocabulary of contemporary liberal political thought. Begin with a conception of society as a system of cooperation for mutual advantage. Society is legitimate when the criterion of mutual advantage is broadly satisfied (versus, say, a situation in which the government or some group systematically coerces some for the sake of others). When society meets the standard of broad legitimacy, each citizen has a duty to do his or her fair share to sustain the social arrangements from which all benefit, and society is justified in using its coercive power when necessary to ensure the performance of this duty. That legitimate society coercion may include mandatory military service in the nation's defense.

A counterargument urged by the late political philosopher Robert Nozick suggests that we typically do not consent to the social benefits we receive and that the involuntary receipt of benefits does not trigger a duty to contribute. Mill anticipated, and rejected, that thesis, insisting that the duty to contribute does not rest on a social contract or voluntarist account of social membership. Besides, the argument Socrates imputes to the Laws in the *Crito* is a compelling one: if a society is not a prison, if as an adult you remain when you have the choice to leave, then you have in fact accepted the benefits, along with whatever burdens the principle of social reciprocity may impose.

Economist Robert Litan has recently suggested that citizens should be "required to give something to their country in exchange for the full range of rights to which citizenship entitles them." Responding in a quasi-libertarian vein, public policy expert Bruce Chapman charges that this proposal has "no moral justification." Linking rights to concrete responsibilities is "contrary to the purposes for which [the United States] was founded and has endured." This simply is not true. For example, the right to receive GI Bill benefits is linked to the fulfillment of military duties. Even the right to vote (and what could be more central to citizenship than that?) rests on law-abidingness; many states disenfranchise convicted felons for extended periods. As Litan points out, this linkage is hardly tyrannical moralism. Rather, it reflects the bedrock reality that "the rights we enjoy are not free" and that it takes real work—contributions from citizens—to sustain constitutional institutions.

Conscription as slavery. Now on to the main event. Posner contends that "Conscription could be described as a form of slavery, in the sense that a conscript is a person deprived of the ownership of his own labor." If slavery is immoral, so is the draft. In a similar vein, Nozick once contended that "taxation of earnings from labor is on a par with forced labor." (If Nozick were right, then the AVF that Posner supports, funded as it is with tax dollars, could also be described as on a par with forced labor.)

Both Posner's and Nozick's arguments prove too much. If each individual's ownership of his or her own labor is seen as absolute, then society as such becomes impossible, because no political community can operate without resources, which must ultimately come from *someone*. Public choice theory predicts, and all of human history proves, that no polity of any size can subsist through voluntary contributions alone; the inevitable free riders must be compelled by law, backed by force, to ante up.

Posner might object, reasonably enough, that this argument illustrates the difference between taxation and conscription: while political community is inconceivable without taxation, it is demonstrably sustainable without conscription. It is one thing to restrict self-ownership of labor out of necessity, but a very different matter to restrict it out of choice. The problem is that this argument proves too little. Posner concedes that "there are circumstances in which military service is an obligation of citizenship." But there are no circumstances in which slavery is an obligation of citizenship. Moreover, it is not morally impermissible to volunteer for military service. But it is impermissible, and rightly forbidden, to voluntarily place oneself in slavery. Therefore, slavery and military service differ in kind, not degree. And if there are circumstances in which military service is an obligation of citizenship, then the state is justified in enforcing that obligation through conscription, which is not impermissible forced labor, let alone a form of slavery. QED. For the purposes of this article, then, I will suppose that a legitimate government would not be exceeding its rightful authority if it chose to move toward a more mandatory system of military recruitment.

Celebrating the cash nexus: four thought experiments. But this is not the end of the argument, because Posner has another arrow in his quiver. He rejects the claim, advanced by Michael Sandel and other communitarians, that substituting market for nonmarket services represents a degrading "commodification" of social and civic life. Indeed, Posner celebrates what communitarians deplore. "Commodification promotes prosperity," he informs us, "and prosperity alleviates social ills." Moreover, commodification enables individuals to transform burdensome obligations into bearable cash payments: middle-aged couples can purchase both care for their children and assisted living for their parents, and so forth.

Posner charges that communitarian theory is incapable of drawing a line between matters that rightly belong within the scope of the market and those that do not. Posner's celebration of the cash nexus is exposed to precisely the same objection. Rather than scoring rhetorical points, I will offer a series of examples designed to help delimit the proper sphere of nonmarket relations.

Paying people to obey the law. Suppose we offered individuals a "compliance bonus"—a cash payment at the end of each year completed without being convicted of a felony or significant misdemeanor. It is not hard to imagine situations in which the benefits of this policy (measured in reduced enforcement costs) would outweigh the outlays for bonuses. What (if anything) is wrong with this?

My answer: at least two things. First, it alters for the worse the expressive meaning of law. In a legitimate order, criminal law represents an authoritative declaration of the behavior the members of society expect of one another. The authoritativeness of the law is supposed to be a sufficient condition for obeying it, and internalizing the sense of law as authoritative is supposed to be a sufficient motive for obedience. To offer compliance payments is to contradict the moral and motivation sufficiency of the law.

Second, payment for compliance constitutes a moral version of Gresham's law: lower motives will tend to drive out higher, and the more comfortable to drive out the more demanding. When those who are inclined to obey the law for its own sake see others receiving compensation, they are likely to question the reasonableness of their conduct and to begin thinking of themselves as suckers. Most would end up accepting payment and coming to resemble more closely those who began by doing so.

Paying citizens for jury duty. Consider the analogy (or disanalogy) between national defense and domestic law enforcement. The latter is divided into two subcategories: voluntary service (there is no draft for police officers) and mandatory service (e.g., jury duty). Our current system of military manpower is all "police" and no "jury." If we conducted domestic law enforcement on our current military model we'd have what might be called "The All-Volunteer Jury," in which we'd pay enough to ensure a steady flow of the jurors the law enforcement system requires to function. There are two compelling reasons not to move in this direction. First, citizens who self-select for jury duty are unlikely to be representative of the population as a whole. Individuals who incur high opportunity costs (those who are gainfully employed, for example) would tend not to show up. The same considerations that militate against forced exclusion of racial and ethnic groups from jury pools should weigh equally against voluntary self-exclusion based upon income or employment status. (We should ask ourselves why these considerations do not apply to the composition of the military.)

Second, it is important for all citizens to understand that citizenship is an *office*, not just a *status*. As an office, citizenship comprises matters of both rights and duties—indeed, some matters that are both. Service on juries is simultaneously a right, in the sense that that there is a strong presumption against exclusion, and a duty, in the sense that there is a strong presumption against evasion. To move jury duty into the category of voluntary, compensated acts would be to remove one of the last reminders that citizenship is more than a legal status.

Paying foreigners to do our fighting for us. Consider: we might do as well or better to hire foreigners (the All-Mercenary Armed Forces) as kings and princes did regularly during the eighteenth century. The cost might well be lower and the military performance just as high. Besides, if we hire foreigners to pick our grapes, why not hire them to do our fighting? There is of course a practical problem, discussed by Machiavelli among others: a pure cash nexus suggests the mercenaries' openness to opportunistic side-switching in response to a better offer, as happened in Afghanistan. In addition, what Abraham Lincoln called the "last full measure of devotion" would be less likely to be forthcoming in the handful of extreme situations in which it is required.

Beyond these practical considerations lies a moral intuition: even if a mercenary army were reliable and effective, it would be wrong, even shameful, to use our wealth to get noncitizens to do our fighting for us. This is something we ought to do for ourselves, as a self-respecting people. I want to suggest that a similar moral principle does some real work in the purely domestic sphere, among citizens.

Paying other citizens to do our fighting for us. Consider military recruitment during the Civil War. In April 1861 President Lincoln called for, and quickly received, 75,000 volunteers. But the expectation of a quick and easy Union victory was soon dashed, and the first conscription act was passed in March 1863. The act contained two opt-out provisions: an individual facing conscription could pay a fee of $300 to avoid a specific draft notice; and an individual could avoid service for the entire war by paying a substitute to volunteer for three years.

This law created a complex pattern of individual incentives and unanticipated social outcomes, such as anti-conscription riots among urban workers. Setting these aside, was there anything wrong in principle with these opt-out provisions? I think so. In the first place, there was an obvious distributional unfairness: the well-off could afford to avoid military service, while the poor and working class could not. Second, even if income and wealth had been more nearly equal, there would have been something wrong in principle with the idea that dollars could purchase exemption from an important civic duty.

The Legacy of the AVF: Economic and Social Stratification

We can now ask: what is the difference between the use of personal resources to opt *out* of military service and the impact of personal resources on the decision to opt *in?* My answer: as both a practical and a moral matter, less than the defenders of the current system would like to believe. To begin with, the decision to implement an AVF has had a profound effect on the educational and class composition of the US military. During World War II and the Korean War—indeed, through the early 1960s—roughly equal percentages of high school and college graduates saw military service, and about one third of college graduates were in the enlisted (that is, non-officer) ranks. Today, enlisted men and women are rarely college graduates, and elite colleges other than the service academies are far less likely to produce military personnel of any rank, officer or enlisted. As a lengthy *New York Times* feature story recently put it, today's military "mirrors a working-class America." Of the first twenty-eight soldiers to die in Iraq, only one came from a family that could be described as well-off.

Many have argued that this income skew is a virtue, not a vice, because the military extends good career opportunities to young men and women whose prospects are otherwise limited. There is something to this argument, of course. But the current system purchases social mobility at the expense of social integration. Today's privileged young people tend to grow up hermetically sealed from the rest of society. Episodic volunteering in soup kitchens does not really break the seal. Military service is one of the few experiences that can.

In an evocative letter to his sons, Brookings Institution scholar Stephen Hess reflects on his experiences as a draftee and defends military service as a vital socializing experience for children from fortunate families. His argument is instructive: "Being forced to be the lowest rank . . . , serving for long enough that you can't clearly see 'the light at the end of the tunnel,' is as close as you will ever come to being a member of society's underclass. To put it bluntly, you will feel in your gut what it means to be at the bottom of the heap. . . . Why should you want to be deprived of your individuality? You shouldn't, of course. But many people are, and you should want to know how this feels, especially if you someday have some responsibility over the lives of other people." It is a matter not just of compassion, but of respect: "The middle class draftee learns to appreciate a lot of talents (and the people who have them) that are not part of the lives you have known, and, after military duty, will know again for the rest of your lives. This will come from being thrown together with—and having to depend on—people who are very different from you and your friends."

A modern democracy, in short, combines a high level of legal equality with an equally high level of economic and social stratification. It is far from inevitable, or even natural, that democratic leaders who are drawn disproportionately from the upper ranks of society will adequately understand the experiences or respect the contributions of those from the lower. Integrative experiences are needed to bring this about. In a society in which economic class largely determines residence and education and in which the fortunate will not willingly associate with the rest, only nonvoluntary institutions cutting across class lines can hope to provide such experiences. If some kind of sustained mandatory service does not fill this bill, it is hard to see what will.

The Importance of Universal Service

The inference I draw from this analysis is far from original: to the extent that circumstances permit, we should move toward a system of universal eighteen-month service for all high school graduates (and in the case of dropouts, all eighteen-year-olds) who are capable of performing it. Within the limits imposed by whatever ceiling is imposed on military manpower, those subject to this system would be able to choose between military and full-time civilian service. (If all military slots are filled, then some form of civilian service would be the only option.) The cost of fully implementing this proposal (a minimum of $60 billion per year) would certainly slow the pace of implementation and might well impose a permanent ceiling on the extent of implementation. The best response to these constraints would be a lottery to which all are exposed and from which none except those unfit to serve can escape.

It might be argued that a program of this sort would have little if any effect on the armed forces, which would continue to draw their manpower from the current stream of volunteers. That may be the case if the military does not expand during the next decade.

But there are reasons to believe that it will. It is fast becoming evident that that the postwar occupation of Iraq will take more troops and last longer than administration officials had predicted. As an interim response, the military has already moved away from the all-volunteer principle. The US Marine Corps has frozen enlistments for all of the 175,000 personnel currently on active duty. Marines whose period of voluntary enlistment has expired are required to remain in the service, on active duty, until the freeze expires. Other services have imposed similar if more limited freezes. It is likely, moreover, that the prospect of being sent to Iraq as part of a vulnerable long-term occupation force will depress voluntary enlistments, especially in the Army and Marines.

There is evidence suggesting that movement toward a less purely voluntary system of military and civilian service could pass the test of democratic legitimacy. For example, a 2002 survey sponsored by the Center for Information and Research on Civic Learning and Engagement (CIRCLE) found 60 percent-plus support for such a move across lines of gender, race and ethnicity, partisan affiliation, and ideology. Still, it is plausible that intense opposition on the part of young adults and their parents could stymie such a change. Assuming that this is the case, there are some feasible interim steps that could yield civic rewards. Let me mention just two.

First, we could follow the advice of former secretary of the navy John Lehman and eliminate the current bias of military recruiters in favor of career personnel and against those willing to serve for shorter periods. As Lehman puts it, we should "actively seek to attract the most talented from all backgrounds with service options that allow them to serve their country . . . without having to commit to six to ten years' active duty." He makes a strong case that this change would markedly increase the number of young men and women from elite colleges and universities who would be willing to undergo military service.

Second, the Congress could pass legislation sponsored by senators John McCain (R-AZ) and Evan Bayh (D-IN) that would dramatically expand Americorps (the Clinton-era national and community service program) from its current level of 50,000 to 250,000 full-time volunteers each year. Survey evidence shows overwhelming (80 percent-plus) support for the basic tenet of this program, that young people should have the opportunity to serve full-time for a year or two and earn significant post-service benefits that can be used for higher education and advanced technical training. As Senator McCain rightly puts it, "one of the curious truths of our era is that while opportunities to serve ourselves have exploded . . . [,] opportunities to spend some time serving our country have dwindled." In this context, the ongoing resistance to Americorps in some quarters of Congress verges on incomprehensible.

It would be wrong to oversell the civic benefits that might accrue from the revisions to the AVF that I propose, let alone the more modest steps I have just sketched. Still, some of our nation's best social scientists see a link between World War II-era military service and that generation's subsequent dedication to our nation's civic life. If reconsidering a decision about military manpower made three decades ago could yield even a fraction of this civic improvement, it would be well worth the effort.

This chapter appeared previously in *Philosophy & Public Policy Quarterly*, vol. 23, no. 3 (Summer 2003).

Sources

The Gallup Poll referred to is cited by Robin Toner in "Trust in the Military Heightens Among Baby Boomers' Children," *New York Times* (May 27, 2003); Richard Posner, "An Army of the Willing," *New Republic* (May 9, 2003); John Stuart Mill, *On Liberty* (Viking, 1982). Robert Litan's arguments for compulsory service occur in, among other sources, "September 11, 2001: The Case for Universal Service," Brookings Review (Fall 2002) and Bruce Chapman's response, "A Bad Idea Whose Time Is Past: The Case Against Universal Service," in the same issue. David M. Halbfinger and Steven A. Holmes, "Military Mirrors Working Class America," *New York Times* (March 30, 2003); Stephen Hess, "Military Service and the Middle Class: A Letter to My Sons," in *United We Serve; National Service and the Future of Citizenship*, edited by E. J. Dionne Jr., Kayla Meltzer Drogosz, and Robert E. Litan (Brookings, 2003). John Lehman's editorial, "Military Recruiting and Common Sense," has been reprinted variously; for instance, see: www.nwaonline.net/pdfarchive/2003/january/28/1-28-03%20A6.pdf. Senator John McCain, "Putting the 'National' in National Service," also has been variously reprinted; see for instance http://www.washingtonmonthly.com/features/2001 /0110.mccain.html (the online edition of the *Washington Monthly*, October 2001).

Conscription—No

Robert K. Fullinwider

In his brief for restoring military conscription, Bill Galston attributes to the All-Volunteer Force two significant civic costs. The all-volunteer policy of raising military forces permits the flourishing of citizenship-without-responsibility, he claims, and "has contributed to a widening gap between the orientation and experience of military personnel and that of the citizenry as a whole."

As to the second cost, Galston misidentifies its cause. An "experience gap" is a function of numbers. If a large proportion of Americans serves under arms decade after decade, eventually a large percentage of the civilian population will have military experience. If a very small number serves, an "experience gap" will become a prominent feature of the civilian world. It doesn't matter what mechanism—conscription or volunteering—generates the big or small numbers. Currently, the military takes in 250,000 recruits a year. Given our total population of 290 million, this intake (and consequent outflow) is miniscule. Small force size is the cause of any present and future "experience gap."

As to the first cost, why does Galston impute it to the all-volunteer policy of military recruitment? There are any number of historical and structural features of American life that might lead some young Americans to believe citizenship is duty-free or to endorse military action too casually. However, suppose the existence of the AVF does contribute to these outcomes. Despite this unfortunate side effect, the soundness of the all-volunteer policy is determined by its effectiveness in producing a first-class military force, and Galston concedes that on this score the all-volunteer policy has been an "impressive" success.

Nevertheless, he wants, while preserving "the gains [in military effectiveness] over the past thirty years," to tamper with the all-volunteer policy by "enlist[ing] the military more effectively in the cause of civic renewal." He would reinstate conscription and make it universal for eighteen-year-olds, although he leaves vague the operational details of the new policy of forced service and the effects it would have on the uniformed services. These details and effects matter a lot, as I will show below.

Philosophical Foundations

Galston also provides a philosophical defense of the government's resorting to coerced service. Against Richard Posner's paean to the libertarian state, Galston quotes John Stuart Mill:

> Everyone who receives the protection of society owes a return for the benefit, and the fact of living in society renders it indispensable that each should be bound to observe a certain line of conduct toward the rest. This conduct consists, first in not injuring the interests of one another . . . and, secondly, in each person's bearing his share . . . of the labors and sacrifices incurred for defending the society or its members from injury and molestation.

From these propositions, it is not hard to draw the same conclusion Galston draws: society may legitimately coerce military service *in the nation's defense.* I agree that society may do so when such coercion is necessary. However, under current circumstances, our nation's military defense is being met without coercion. Coercion would add nothing to it. In fact, the universal service scheme Galston proposes reaches far beyond the simple propositions Mill adduces on behalf of conscription to defend "society or its members from injury and molestation." Galston needs premises that support *conscription to promote a social experiment.* Why? Because almost all of those conscripted under his plan will end up working in some inner-city homeless shelter or tutoring first-graders in reading or engaging in some similar task that by no stretch of the imagination can be called "defense of the nation." In being forced to undertake these "duties," young people will learn, Galston hopes, that citizenship is not free and that rights bring respon-sibilities. Moreover, they will experience a kind of "civic socialization," the rich and privileged sons and daughters of America no longer "hermetically sealed from the rest of society" but laboring alongside the lower classes. For a brief time in forced service, upper-, middle-, and lower-class kids will experience intensely a kind of equality they will not know most of their lives. However, that this forced service will actually civically profit those who bear it or successfully teach the right lessons in responsibility is highly speculative. This is why I said Galston needs a philosophical defense not of conscription to defend the nation but of conscription to promote a social experiment.

Practical Difficulties

Galston limns military service as one of the few experiences that can yield the civic socializing he wants, but a close reading of his essay shows that military service is *not* what his coerced servers will be experiencing. He proposes, ideally, a universal draft of eighteen-year-olds. The draftees can choose between military or civilian service. However, if all military slots are already filled, he notes parenthetically, then civilian service will be the only option available to new conscripts.

Now, since the military services have met their accession needs over the last two decades through volunteers, a coercive universal service scheme piggybacked onto the present system would seem to yield no increase in military experience and, thus, no increase in egalitarian shoulder-rubbing. Of course, no coercive scheme can actually be piggybacked onto the present system without *altering* it, and that is why Galston needs to put some operational details of his draft on the table and discuss their effects.

If we are to have the draft Galston envisages, here are some basic changes we might expect. First, we have to reconstitute the central bureaucracy of the Selective Service System and reestablish the roughly four thousand local draft boards around the country. Second, we have to be prepared to put people in jail. For good reasons and silly ones, plenty of conscripts will resist. Their resistance cannot be allowed to succeed if the whole coercive scheme is not to be undermined. Third, we have to be prepared for gender inequities. Suppose there were some slots in the military the new draftees could take. Those slots could be filled only on an 8 to 1 ratio, men to women. This ratio represents the current gender configuration of the military and no one in the services or Congress wants to change it. Under Galston's draft, some women will complain that they are disproportionately and unfairly excluded from their preferred choice, military service.

Fourth, we have to be prepared to put in place a set of exemptions and deferments. Galston insists that only the unfit (physically and mentally) will be exempted from service under his plan, but this is surely not feasible (and further, this exempted group itself will turn out to be very large if *military* standards are imposed; the single largest group of young men of draft-age who did not serve in the Vietnam War era were those who failed their preinduction physicals). For example, a new high school graduate may be an unmarried mother of a small child or the financial mainstay of a household with ill or disabled parents or a crucial income-earner in a family already below the poverty line. There can be no politically feasible conscription that does not exempt on the basis of hardship (and it is worth recalling that ten times as many young men received hardship exemptions from the Vietnam draft as received student deferments). There will be clamor for other exemptions, as well. For example, young Mormons go on extended tours of foreign missionary work after high school; Congress will undoubtedly be asked by the Mormon Church to exempt these young people from Galston's draft or at least defer their service. Other groups will make their claims, as well.

More important from the military's point of view will be the way in which a draft will threaten enlistment standards. Galston asserts that the AVF policy has had a profound effect on the educational composition of the services and he is right, but not in the way he suggests. The eighteen-year-olds recruited into today's military are far better educated than their civilian counterparts. This is because the military can be selective. It can turn away not only unqualified but *minimally* qualified applicants and accept only those who meet a much higher standard. Newspaper stories periodically observe that the AVF has to work hard to meet its recruiting goals. What the stories don't mention is that the services have to work hard because they set their standards so high. They recruit, with few exceptions, only high school graduates, and among those, the services look for kids who score above average on the Armed Forces Qualifying Test (more than two-thirds of enlistees do). The services would have far less trouble recruiting if they lowered standards—especially if they lowered them to the level prevailing in the conscription years Galston looks back on fondly. And lower its standards the military might have to do if Galston's conscription plan goes into effect. If the new conscripts are to be given a choice of service, military or civilian, it will be politically difficult to deny the military option to those who are *minimally* (though not exceptionally) qualified to serve.

The Real Message of Coerced Service

As part of his philosophical defense of coerced service, Galston notes the expressive dimension of the law. The law not only tells us what to do, it sends messages as well. What message will Galston's draft send? It won't be the message World War II conscription sent. In World War II, America was in a fight to the death against fascism in both its German and Japanese variants. Between 1941 and 1945, 10 million men were drafted and 20 million served overall—this out of a national population of 140 million. The great majority of able-bodied men under thirty bore arms. Those who remained on the home front—men, women, and children—did their part. Women went into the factories; children collected scrap. Everyone submitted to rationing and regimentation. Consequently, the conscription law's expressive effect was unmistakably a message of social duty and needed sacrifice.

Galston's draft law is unlikely to send any such message because its rationale is so transparently didactic. He, with his law, will more likely come across as a meddling busybody, disdaining the life courses young adults might choose for themselves (with civic and service components incorporated in any number of legitimate ways) and insisting that all of them submit to the particular pattern the government thinks best for their civic souls.

Galston claims to eschew any policy like the Vietnam-era draft. This is a wise move, since that draft was thoroughly discredited by the time it ended in 1973. However, the basic flaw in that draft was not that it gave some college kids deferments or led to an active force skewed toward the lower middle classes. Indeed, the Vietnam-era draft had far fewer loopholes than the 1950s draft Galston admires. (For example, Galston notes that the conscription of the 1950s brought college graduates into the enlisted ranks, thus producing the social mixing he desires. However, he doesn't say how many of these graduates stayed in uniform and for how long. In the 1950s, a drafted college graduate could get right back out of the service by teaching in a public school, and some not insubstantial number did.)

What discredited the Vietnam-era draft more than anything else was its expressive content. Let me explain. By 1968, although America's active-duty military numbered 3.6 million, Selective Service was filling slots from a national population of 200 million, a population disproportionately bulging right at the youth end, as the leading edge of the baby boom was slamming its way through high school. Nearly 27 million men came of draft age during the Vietnam War but 16 million of them—more than half—never served at all. Of that number, 4 million were lottery escapees—men put in the lottery pool after 1969 but lucky enough to possess lottery numbers that excluded them from the annual draft calls. (Incidentally, these lottery escapees amounted to eight times the number of college kids given student deferments.) Small draft calls from a large target population made conscription look not like a mechanism of universal service but like a booby prize for the unlucky few. *That* was the expressive effect of the Vietnam-era draft.

If a draft is to teach a lesson in universal duty, it needs to approach universality itself, as it did in World War II and in the early stages of the Cold War. This is no doubt why Galston wants to conscript all eighteen-year-olds. However, he concedes that shanghaiing into service a sizeable portion of the 4 million kids who turn eighteen each year might dampen voter enthusiasm for a fully universal conscription. "The best response" to this state of affairs, writes Galston, is limited conscription using a lottery—in other words, the best response is reinstating the very feature of the Vietnam-era draft that divided youth into the unlucky few and the lucky many.

Conscription Properly Bounded

Galston suggests that the country's current military engagements may require more manpower than current enlistments provide. If manpower shortages arise, the military will be loathe to return to a draft until other options fail. The impressive success of the AVF that Galston refers to arises out of three facts—first, that the men and women who make up the services' platoons, companies, and battalions want to be there; second, that they are well-educated, committed, disciplined, and trainable; and third, that they serve long enough to become highly proficient at their jobs. The American military is an expeditionary force, designed to fight overseas, using complex weaponry and sophisticated tactics. Even in the infantry, it needs soldiers who can master an array of technical tasks. Short-termers (which is what draftees would be) would barely learn their craft before finishing their active duty. Moreover, nothing undermines unit morale and cohesion like the presence of malcontents, troublemakers, and malingerers—and a draft will deliver up plenty of each. Under conscription, the Army cannot reward bad behavior with a discharge—otherwise coerced service wouldn't work. It has to keep bad eggs in the barracks or in the brig.

Even so, if the Army truly needs not 70,000 but 140,000 or 280,000 recruits a year and can't meet this need through voluntary enlistments, then the country may have to resort to a draft. It might be a draft short on the civic lessons desired by Galston but it would be one justified on the grounds set out by Mill.

Further, if the country decides that defense against domestic terror attacks requires the creation of a substantial new homeland "light" military force (e.g., soldiers trained to stand guard around every nuclear power plant, chemical factory, airport, train station, power grid, hydroelectric dam, hospital, and government office in the country), then something approaching universal conscription might be appropriate. The point is, the question of conscription should be settled on grounds of national defense, not determined by hoped-for civic by-products.

Postscript: A Comment on Class

Galston laments the absence of the college-educated from the ranks. Privileged youth currently escape the burden of service, he says, and this is bad for America.

Others likewise see the AVF through the prism of "class." Unfortunately, much of the discussion of the military's class structure is built on an implicit class bias. For example, consider a recent policy report by Marc Magee and Steven J. Nider, "Citizen Soldiers and the War on Terror," for the Progressive Policy Institute. In their report, Magee and Nider praise legislation passed last year that will make available a "citizen soldier" option in which individuals can enlist for an eighteen-month tour of duty in one of the armed services and then serve a further period in the Individual Ready Reserves, the Peace Corps, or Americorps.

The new short-term option, Magee and Nider believe, "would appeal especially to college-educated youths, who are now dramatically underrepresented in" the military.

The creation of a citizen soldier enlistment track marks the most important change in America's military recruitment policies since the draft was ended. The introduction of the all-volunteer force in 1974 ushered in an era of military recruitment that targeted people primarily interested in cash, job security, or technical training. The citizen soldier track adds a civic dimension to this economic model.

Instead of using a recruitment strategy "based exclusively on economic incentives," write Magee and Nider, the new track will allow "the nation's most fortunate sons and daughters" to act on their duty to contribute to America's defense.

Here we see the germs of a charge that has been thrown at the AVF since its beginnings—that it amounts to a "mercenary" force. (One recent example: John Gregory Dunne, essayist and novelist, gives voice in the May 29, 2003 issue of the *New York Review of Books* to the claim that the AVF is a "Hessian force of the unlettered and underprivileged.") Do we want people to do our fighting who enter service motivated exclusively by the prospect of financial gain? That's how mercenary armies are formed. Can we honor what Magee and Nider call our "civic ethic of equal sacrifice" by turning the job of defense over to mere hired hands?

This "mercenary" charge has been around since the AVF was created. What merit does it have? None. It is true that military pay was raised after the draft ended, because military recruiters had to begin competing in an open job market. Today, a private in the Army with less than two years service earns almost $1,100 a month basic pay. Factor in the free food, housing, and medical care he receives by living on base, and this is not a bad income for a twenty-year-old with only a high school diploma. Moreover, the private may get an up-front cash bonus for enlisting and be eligible to receive quite substantial college tuition benefits at the end of his term. All in all, the military offers an attractive option for many youth. But this is not an option open to the truly "unlettered and underprivileged." As we've already seen, the services set a high bar for admission. Those who fill the enlisted ranks of the AVF come principally from lower middle- and middle-class blue collar and white collar families. They are high school graduates with good grades, with good entry-test scores, and capable of college work. Indeed, many of those who leave service after their initial term of enlistment go straight on for a baccalaureate using the tuition benefits they've earned.

A decent wage and prospects of future financial rewards: do these make a recruit a mercenary? Where is the evidence that no "civic dimension" weighs in the choices of current recruits? Where is the evidence that enlistees in the AVF are motivated "exclusively" by financial inducements rather than by a mix of patriotic feeling, desire for adventure, and a wish for an occupation both socially meaningful and personally challenging, all of this leavened by an attractive economic package to boot? Where is the evidence that members of the AVF are Hessians who would abandon their Army, Air Force, or Navy jobs to serve in the Canadian, Libyan, German, Venezuelan, or Chinese armies for higher wages and bonuses? There is none. Indeed, the "mercenary" charge is not an induction from empirical evidence, and never has been, but a deduction from unstated prejudices. The deduction moves from the fact that economic incentives offered by the military play a role in enlistments to the conclusion that enlistees are mercenaries. There's a missing premise here. What is it? That people for whom economic incentives make a difference are mercenaries? This can hardly be the right premise, as the report by Magee and Nider so ironically illustrates. After initially characterizing the AVF policy as targeting people "primarily interested" in money and relying "exclusively on economic incentives," they extol the new "citizen soldier" option that will, they hope, appeal to upper middle-class and college-educated youth. Part of that appeal, however, turns out to be *cash*—a $5,000 cash bonus or an $18,000 education grant to pay off tuition loans! Now, if upper-class youth aren't turned into mercenaries by accepting substantial bundles of cash, how are lower middle-class youth nevertheless compromised by the military's financial compensation packages?

Consider this further fact. The military maintains a substantial officer corps, largely composed of graduates from the service academies or from college ROTC programs. These graduates are not individuals who've taken a vow of poverty. The cadets and midshipmen at the academies gain a free college education; many ROTC students receive substantial scholarships. A newly commissioned lieutenant begins with more than twice the basic pay of a private. While a master sergeant with fifteen years' experience and a family of four takes home $53,000 in RMC (regular military compensation, which includes basic pay, food and housing allowances, and tax advantages), a lieutenant colonel with fifteen years' experience and a family of four takes home $95,000. To the critics of the AVF like Magee and Nider, the sergeant is part of a tainted volunteer system relying "exclusively" or "primarily" on economic incentives. Yet, except for rare moments in our history, the officer corps has always been all-volunteer. If the sergeant is a mercenary, why then isn't the lieutenant colonel a super-mercenary? The critics of the AVF never draw this conclusion. Why not? It begins to look like the missing premise in the "mercenary" argument is some piece of class snobbery: for lower-class kids the money is all that counts, while for upper-class kids the money merely eases the way for them to act on selfless motives of service and duty. What else explains the dual attitude Magee and Nider take toward the regular enlistee and the "citizen soldier," the latter drawn (they hope) from "the ranks of the best educated and most well-off citizens," while the former comes from an average American family?

Magee and Nider, like many critics of the AVF, focus on the enlisted ranks and then treat them as the whole military. For example, they claim that college-educated youth are dramatically underrepresented in the AVF. However, the college-educated are underrepresented only in the enlisted ranks, not in the officer corps. Nearly every commissioned officer is a college graduate. Magee and Nider lament the fact that only 6.5 percent of active duty enlistees have had some college experience, by contrast to 46 percent of the general population. However, when you add in the officer corps, the percentage of active-duty military personnel *in total* with some college experience jumps to 21 percent. Indeed, 15 percent of the military have a bachelor's degree or higher, a figure not terribly out of line with the civilian world, where 26 percent of individuals twenty-five or older possess at least a baccalaureate.

The low percentage of bachelor's degrees in the enlisted ranks is a matter of concern only if we think the military will perform better by having college-trained privates and corporals serving under high-school-educated sergeants. Even Galston's universal draft wouldn't supply the services with more college-educated privates, only more college-bound ones.

This chapter appeared previously in *Philosophy & Public Policy Quarterly*, vol. 23, no. 3 (Summer 2003).

Sources

Demographic data taken from Table 1, "Age and Sex: 2000," *United States: 2000: Summary Population and Housing Characteristics*, Part 1 (Washington, DC: US Census Bureau, November 2002), p. 2; and "Educational Attainment in the United States," Report P20-536 (Washington, DC: US Census Bureau, December 2000). Data about characteristics of manpower in the services is drawn from the *Defense Almanac* <www.defenselink.mil/pub/almanac>. On the military recruitment standards and the qualities of current recruits, see Charles Abell, Principal Deputy Undersecretary of Defense for Manpower and Readiness, "Media Roundtable on Personnel and Readiness Issues," *Defense Link*, December 23, 2002 <www.defenselink.mil/news/Dec2002/t12232002caq.html>. For military pay, see "Military Compensation: Monthly Basic Pay Table - January 1, 2003" <http://militarypay.dtic.mill/pay/bp/paytables/Jan2003.htmb> and "Military Pay: Regular Military Compensation Calculator" <http://militarypay.dtic.mil/militarypay/cgi-bin/rmc.pl>. For details of the Vietnam-era draft, see Lawrence M. Baskir and William A. Strauss, *Chance and Circumstance: The Draft, the War, and the Vietnam Generation* (New York: Vintage Books, 1978), esp. pp. 20–22. The "citizen soldier" option is discussed by Marc Magee and Steven J. Nider, "Policy Report: Citizen Soldiers and the War on Terror" (Washington, DC: Progressive Policy Institute, December 2002). The remark by John Gregory Dunne is in "The Horror is Seductive," *New York Review of Books*, 50 (May 29, 2003), p. 23.

Conscription: Between the Horns

Mick Womersley

In the previous two chapters William A. Galston and Robert K. Fullinwider engaged in debate on the merits of conscription. The day after I read their competing articles for the first time, Internet service provider America Online (AOL) carried on its "Welcome Page" the following headline, "Is war worth 87 million? Bush tells us we must sacrifice." Although the presidential speech the previous weekend had concentrated on monetary sacrifice, other more important sacrifices are asked for. The night I read the articles posted on AOL I realized that it was the first time in a while that I did not see another one, two, or three portraits of dead US servicemen that typically end the nightly news program, the Jim Lehrer "Newshour." Since these memorials put a human face into what might otherwise be a dry and academic debate, it is appropriate to begin a deliberation of Galston's proposal for universal service conscription with consideration of the faces involved.

I doubt that I am the only person in the United States who is sick at heart to witness this regular and morbid parade of dead youth across our screens. One learns from the accompanying captions that they are primarily of blue collar and rural extraction, and for the most part are barely out of their teenage years. This is extremely sad. Yet more dismaying perhaps is that some *are* older. These would be the fathers. One or two in their fifties are possibly grandfathers. The earlier pictures of young women killed were harder still to bear.

These are men and women who have entered the service of their country in what is probably for most a commendable attempt at self-improvement tempered by a strong ethic of public service. They are engaged in a very difficult mission devised by an administration remarkably impenetrable to civil debate. They are posted in a hostile country with a bad climate many thousands of miles from home—in many cases away from their own young families. That some of them are injured while others are killed is a consideration that seems to me to outweigh all others. Whatever our beliefs about the war, they are dying in our service. This mortality is *not*, as some eminently liberal Washingtonian friends opposed to the war recently tried to convince me over dinner, entirely an occupational hazard related to the freely chosen profession of the people involved. The wounding and dying is not some failure of OSHA's occupational safety regulations or a regrettable workplace accident of some other kind, but instead is, or should be, the closest thing to sacred that a secular state could observe. We recruited them, taking advantage of their economic vulnerability. We *put* them in harm's way. Their harm or death, is, or should be, a deliberate and careful act of sacrificial self-defense on the part of a threatened democratic state. (If it is not, then the deaths of more than a thousand American and British troops and civilians, and those of thousands of Iraqis and others, now should weigh on the consciences of the authors of the war.)

The Unfair Burden

If my words seem overly passionate, there is reason for it. I have some personal experience with all this. Enlisting at seventeen in the British Royal Air Force, for more than six years I served in comparative happiness and fulfillment as an aircraft technician and rescue party leader. Then the government of Margaret Thatcher mounted what seemed to me and most of the folk in my home region a concerted and physically brutal attack on the rights of workers and the unemployed: another "limited war" planned by neoconservatives. When the policy on the European placement of American short-range nuclear missiles provoked a further reaction from feminists and environmentalists, and my own girlfriend was caught "manning" the barricades stormed by police, I was sick at heart. It was time to leave. After pressing my case at a military tribunal, I was permitted an honorable discharge as a conscientious objector. Helping to save lives as a military rescuer, I was able to learn the great value of military service in a just cause. Pressed by conscience into an early discharge, I can easily understand the great individual and collective harm done by compulsion.

I differ, then, from Bob Fullinwider, who seems to believe that it is safe for a democracy not to distribute such sacrifice around more equitably, the usual prescription for which is called a draft. It is also clear, although the administration continues to prevaricate on the point, that fresh forces *are* now needed to relieve the strain on the overburdened regular force. Recent announcements from both the United Kingdom and the United States about adding new forces and further lengthening the tours for both part-time and regular soldiers already in Iraq amply demonstrate the need.

If Britain and the United States must continue to expend both treasure *and* blood in places like Iraq and Afghanistan, it is patently and dangerously unfair that the burden of shedding blood is placed upon middle- and lower-class youth. Yet Bill Galston's plea for a program of universal national service to lessen the injustice is patently unworkable. Even the eighteenth-century political philosopher John Stuart Mill, the authority cited by Galston for the "fair share" argument, would be forced to concede that the monumental disutility created by such a scheme might easily outweigh the utility. Disutilities would occur not only in the minds of those drafted; as Fullinwider points out, our military probably would want only a fraction of the new forces, condemning the rest to some domestic service program, a new and ill-formed Civilian Conservation Corps (CCC), the details of which Galston does not provide. One finds a dilemma: on one horn is a "spectatorial" democracy, in which some merely watch while others serve and die. On the other horn of the dilemma one finds the misuse of the state's powers to coerce all young people into what will clearly become a make-work and vacuous service in homeless shelters, inner-city schools, and the military. Since neither extreme is tolerable, there *must* be some middle ground between the horns.

A Failure to Appreciate Harm

Fullinwider concedes that a draft is legitimate if needed for national defense. But he disputes that a draft is needed now. Additionally, he cites that such interference will no doubt reduce the efficiency and effectiveness of the force, at least in part because it will reduce the overall quality and tractability of recruits. These considerations are the basis for his contention that the All-Volunteer Force (AVF) should be left as is. The personnel recruited must be of good quality; therefore draftees are not welcome. There is no mercenary impulse to worry about, since the people involved know what they are getting into.

But do we know what we are getting into? As an unintended consequence of his defense of the *status quo,* Fullinwider belittles the distinct harm that is done when our volunteers come home to their relatives in aluminum coffins or wheelchairs. It must be extremely hard to explain to some of these parents, wives, husbands, and children that their loves died as a consequence of a career choice. To make it more than that, the civic life of a democratic nation still requires, even in the age of globalization, the perpetuation of the civic myth of democratic service. It is even better if it is not actually a myth. We have to respect military and other national service over and above its career components. Service cannot safely be restricted to elites *or* to lower classes or minorities, since to do so aids in the perpetuation of both. As Galston forcefully argues, service must be spread out over society as evenly as possible.

At the same time, however, Galston fails to appreciate the unequal but distinct harm nonetheless that is done when a sovereign person is compelled in any way. Conscription, whether for the military or a wider range of service options, is compulsion. If it is not slavery, then those who are conscripted are likely to act like slaves in the absence of any better argument for their service; they will be stubborn and intractable. The reason why draftees fought so well in the Second World War and for the early part of the Cold War—and by comparison so poorly in Vietnam—is because they accepted the reasons given for their service and, by extension, the authority of the state and the leaders who sent them. They were not, in most cases, fully compelled, but instead they were quite willing to serve. Because some in the ranks were compelled and unwilling, the Vietnam War was often indifferently fought. The continued willingness of volunteers in Iraq depends in large part on how well their burdens are distributed, and on how strongly they believe in the mission and its progenitors' sincerity. The Bush administration is beginning to see that willingness erode.

Even a nation that enjoys an enduring and vigorous ethic of universal military service might eventually regret the use of universal compulsion for other reasons. Germans who resisted compulsion in the World War II era were likely to find themselves in prison or quickly dead, to the everlasting shame of that state. Willy Brandt, former premier of Germany, would have agreed. He escaped to Norway during World War II, where he resisted German occupation. Following the defeat of Nazism, he became, of course, a hero. The students of the White Rose Resistance, one of very few German anti-war protests in the Second World War, are rightly heroes to their country today, and their story, too rarely told in the United States, demonstrates the extreme nature of the harm from universal compulsion in a time of attenuated conscience. The slogan, "America—love it or leave it" a popular sentiment during the Vietnam War, expressed the contempt of "hawks" for "doves," but the German experience suggests strongly that hawks must be balanced by doves. Both must be allowed to thrive for democracy to endure.

During World War II, Korea, and Vietnam, many American people of conscience—Mennonites, Brethren, Amish, and Quakers—became smokejumpers, farm-workers, firefighters, medics, and mental-health workers, trading horse and buggy for pack and Pulaski and other tools. Pacifists performed alternative service to their honor and that of the nation that had, belatedly, realized the civic value of their conscience and organized Alternative Service. If the German *Reich* had included enough such people (if they hadn't evicted them to America several centuries earlier), it is possible that the Holocaust could have been avoided. A similar, although less well-worked out act of conscience on the part of American youth ended the Vietnam War after My Lai and other disasters brought home the fact that it was the wrong war, in the wrong place, at the wrong time. A system of just civic service must therefore honor service *and* conscience while avoiding compulsion.

A draft is therefore a civic myth: a unicorn. There is no such animal. Democratic service is not achieved by the compulsion of the state, but by the individual consent of those who serve. It will not work to draft youth for a war with which they disagree. They will not fight the war; the war will then be lost. Their disagreement, however, is not something to be hated and despised, as it so often is by conservatives and so-called patriots. It is instead a national treasure of sorts, since it is just that disagreement that can stop a nation that is about to propel itself into an unjust or unnecessary war, as did Nazi Germany in the late 1930s, as did the United States in 1963 and 1964. As we might have done just recently.

Impasse. Fullinwider's solution continues the *status quo,* and the parade of doomed and underprivileged youth continues on nightly news programs. Galston's solution will not work practically, and it encourages stubborn, intractable behavior and discourages protest. Neither is actually tolerable. For myself, I would like to see universality at least sufficient to have President Bush, Secretary of Defense Rumsfeld, Deputy Secretary of Defense Wolfowitz, and the rest pulling guard duty in Baghdad. If they were to be killed, I'd give them the same empty ceremony that is provided to the rest of the returning dead. But this is juvenile pique, venting, mere name-calling. It is not a long-term solution, a solution that will outlast the neoconservatives. And the problem is clearly not "who serves" as much as "who leads."

Between the Horns: Service *and* Education

A route between the horns is mentioned, but not examined fully, by both Galston and Fullinwider. They refer to the system of benefits available for the current volunteer service programs within and without the military. There's a policy that I like! I am a professor at an inexpensive private college that serves students of lower- and middle-class backgrounds, and my students regularly take part in these programs as a way of broadening their horizons and saving money for college. On any given day, one of my classes will contain twenty students, of whom one or possibly two will have served an enlistment in the armed services. One may be an active member of the National Guard, and a much larger number are or have been or will be volunteers for outfits like Americorps, our rural fire department and rescue ambulance, college search and rescue team, or sheriff's department. Recent internships supported by the college have included service as diverse as search and rescue in Yosemite National Park, civic service with nonprofit organizations in Washington, DC, or work with our local food bank. Our students serve, and we are proud of them.

At other times in my college teaching career, I have taught at places where the average incomes of parents were a lot higher and the average esteem for service of any kind much lower. I much prefer my students now. But, without the connections that the wealthy enjoy, in a world of "it's not what you know, but who you know," my students will struggle after college, and they know it, and I hate the thought. I can't abolish the other kinds of schools and other kinds of students, the ones where service is not on the curriculum and where procession through life is assured by connections.

But I want to reduce their effect on society and increase the effect of students like my own. I need a way, as does Galston, to encourage the civic participation of students from deserving backgrounds, a way to train them, and many more of them, to be the leaders of the kind of society in which I want to live. Fullinwider accuses Galston of "social engineering." I agree, and say we need more of it, and better targeted. There's nothing intrinsically wrong with the engineering of incentives; in fact when I was at the University of Maryland's School of Public Policy, more than one of Galston and Fullinwider's eminent colleagues explained at length taxing "bads" and subsidizing goods. To not pay attention to such things, it was quite soberly explained, was to run the risk of perverse results. Perverted results are clearly what we have in a society where we throw off political leadership of the present sort. A long-term solution would replace the leadership pool of society with more deserving characters.

To tax the bad of non-service while sponsoring the good of service, one needs a place to grasp the "monetary handles." That place is college. The route between the horns needs to 1) achieve Galston's goal of reorganizing incentives in society to foster service and civic participation, 2) observe Fullinwider's standards of non-compulsion and noninterference with the AVF, and 3) address my own strong preference for a college system that reduces elitism in society and recognizes service to society. The first step is not the revision of the military or even the Americorps program, but of the Federal Student Aid Program.

Service to government and society in general is best repaid by strong government support for education and career building. Both Galston and Fullinwider refer to the increasing need for education in the armed forces. Revising student aid in favor of service is one way to provide a stronger link between colleges and the military, a link Galston says is sorely needed. Similar beneficiaries would include the Peace Corps, Americorps/VISTA, inner-city and rural schools, hospitals, and environmental and social service providers. Instead of reinstituting Selective Service boards all around the country, I advocate elected national service boards, whose job it would be to distribute financial aid for higher education on the basis of something like a one-to-one distribution, say one year of service to the greater community = one year of support for education and training for young people to progress in life. This is a rate deliberately higher (times three or four) than that offered currently through the GI Bill, in effect a reinforcement of that benefit and its yet further extension to nonmilitary service. Prospective students applying for aid would demonstrate that they have participated in service by producing approved documentation such as records of military service or supporting letters from social service agencies. Aid would go for all kinds of college and university work, but also for technical skills training and the like. A revolving door would be instituted in which high school graduates serve to earn their baccalaureate and then return to service to earn advanced degrees. The accession of graduates to higher posts in civic life, business, and government would create a better understanding of service at that level and ensure fair and just recruitment practices. Nepotism and favor would be steadily eliminated.

One fully intended consequence would be to dramatically increase and ease the pathways by which youth from underprivileged backgrounds become leaders in all walks of life and in society in general. There would be no compulsion, since students are not compelled to take federal financial aid. Students from wealthy families where service is disregarded would not be penalized, but would eventually find it harder to do what they are accustomed to doing: secure college places and jobs denied those with merit. Students from wealthy families who serve meaningfully would be at no disadvantage. But for students from rough and difficult backgrounds, the pathway to success would be much clearer. There would be no harm to persons of conscience, since they would find ample outlet in the various forms of service allowed by the boards. There would be no harm to religious minorities, such as Mormons, cited by Galston, whose elected local boards would presumably adjust to local conditions and, for instance, allow nonreligious missionary service in the overseas clinics already run by that Church.

Possible Objections

Some will argue that this scheme would fail to fulfill the requirements of equality and universality insisted on by Galston. My response: conscription was *never* really universal. People are intrinsically unequal in lots of ways. There were always ways out of the draft, for instance, and many of these loopholes contributed greatly to the dishonesty of individuals and society in general. Were those Vietnam-era draft-dodgers who went to Canada and who were later pardoned by President Carter equal in conscience to the Peace Church youth who went to prison? Was it equal service to be made an army cook at home during World War II, or to be a fighter pilot or marine? Of course not.

One finds intrinsic inequalities among people and their contributions. Requiring equality from life is akin to requiring blood from a stone. Wise people usually settle for justice, best decided by a jury of peers, in this case a national service board. It would be a far more just world if the people who were most likely to die in the next Iraq war were also the people whose expertise and leadership would be sought out after the conflict, if the returning twenty-year-old GIs could become twenty-one-year-old college students, and twenty-five-year-old graduates with good job prospects.

Others will argue that the scheme fails to fulfill the requirement of noninterference with the AVF that is recommended by Fullinwider. I doubt that this will be a problem in practice. It might instead increase the quality and quantity of the pool of applicants upon which the military must draw. In a world where the profession of arms becomes increasingly technical, linking military service directly to college help would probably be a boon. And, as recent events have taught us, we need more troops.

Finally, it might be argued that my scheme reinforces a possible mercenary quality in today's AVF. I disagree. Galston cites Stephen Hess on the social value of serving at low rank with no sign of "light at the end of the tunnel." There's a further applicable fact about tunnel vision in today's youth. For most of our youngsters of the instant-gratification era, the reasons they enlist or take volunteer service will almost certainly be good and wholesome; their time horizon is typically too limited for it to be otherwise. The reward of college support will be known and understood, but as a carrot it will be less attractive compared to the others available: seeing the world, doing adventurous things, making a difference. The stick that drives, of course, is us: their parents and teachers, from whom they wish to be removed as fast as humanly possible.

Conclusion

To summarize my argument: Galston is entirely correct to state that society risks much by ignoring the issue of justice in service institutionalized in the current AVF. The nightly parade of dead, largely lower- and middle-class faces across our screens is a great and terrible harm and a gross injustice. The burdens need to be shared. But Fullinwider is also correct to say that compulsory service can create more harm than good. Instead, we should link service more closely to civic society through far stronger support for education, working at the same time to undercut unearned privilege and create a corps of civic leaders beyond compare in history. That's what we really need, not a draft.

This chapter appeared previously in *Philosophy & Public Policy Quarterly*, vol. 23, no. 4 (Fall 2003).

Sources

William A. Galston, "A Sketch of Argument for Conscription," and Robert K. Fullinwider, "Conscription—No" first appeared in *Philosophy & Public Policy Quarterly*, vol. 23, no. 3 (Summer 2003). The Mennonite, Quaker, and Church of the Brethren are those Christian religious persuasions that hold to the "peace testimony" of conscience against all war. Amish are perhaps best seen as fundamentalist Mennonites. The author is an indifferently observant Quaker.

Index

About the Editor and Contributors

Robert K. Fullinwider is research scholar at the Institute for Philosophy and Public Policy at the School of Public Policy, University of Maryland. Among other topics, he has written on military conscription, affirmative action, war, multicultural education, professional ethics, and moral learning. He is author (with Judith Lichtenberg) of *Leveling the Playing Field: Justice, Politics, and College Admissions* (Rowman & Littlefield, 2004); he is editor of *Public Education in a Multicultural Society* (1996) and *Civil Society, Democracy, and Civic Renewal*. His book *The Reverse Discrimination Controversy* (1980) was a selection of the Lawyer's Literary Guild. During 1996–1998, he was research director for the National Commission on Civic Renewal, a joint project of the Institute for Philosophy and Public Policy and the Pew Charitable Trusts.

William A. Galston is director of the Institute for Philosophy and Public Policy, Saul I. Stern Professor of Civic Engagement at the School of Public Policy at the University of Maryland, and director of the Center for Information and Research on Civic Learning and Engagement (CIRCLE). He is a political theorist who both studies and participates in American politics and domestic policy. He was deputy assistant to the president for Domestic Policy, 1993–1995, and executive director of the National Commission on Civic Renewal, 1996–1999. Galston served as a founding member of the Board of the National Campaign to Prevent

Teen Pregnancy and as chair of the campaign's task force on religion and public values. He is the author of five books and nearly one hundred articles in moral and political theory, American politics, and public policy. His publications include *Liberal Purposes* (Cambridge, 1991), *Liberal Pluralism* (Cambridge, 2002), *The Practice of Liberal Pluralism* (Cambridge, 2005), and *Public Matters: Essays on Politics, Policy, and Religion* (Rowman & Littlefield).

Verna V. Gehring is editor at the Institute for Philosophy and Public Policy at the School of Public Policy, University of Maryland. She is a philosopher broadly interested in the obligations of state and citizen and the various accounts of civil society. In addition to her work on the seventeenth-century political philosopher Thomas Hobbes and his enduring influence, Gehring's interest is applied to such contemporary matters as the state lottery, nuclear proliferation, computer hackers, baseball scandals, and the social harms caused by imposters. She is editor in chief of *Philosophy & Public Policy Quarterly*, coeditor (with William A. Galston) of *Philosophical Dimensions of Public Policy* (2002), and editor of *War after September 11* (2002), *Genetic Prospects: Essays on Biotechnology, Ethics, and Public Policy* (2003), and *The Internet in Public Life* (2004).

Peter Levine (www.peterlevine.ws) is deputy director of CIRCLE, the Center for Information and Research on Civic Learning and Engagement (www.civicyouth.org). CIRCLE conducts and funds research on young people's civic education and participation. Levine is also a research scholar at the Institute for Philosophy and Public Policy in the University of Maryland's School of Public Policy. From 1991 until 1993, he was a research associate at Common Cause, helping that organization to lobby for campaign finance reform and government ethics. In the late 1990s, he was deputy director of the National Commission on Civic Renewal, chaired by Senator Sam Nunn and William Bennett. Levine is also an associate for the Charles Kettering Foundation. He is a cofounder of the Deliberative Democracy Consortium (www. deliberative-democracy.net). Levine is the author of four books. He also co-organized the writing of *The Civic Mission of Schools*, a report released by Carnegie Corporation of New York and CIRCLE in 2003 (www. civicmissionofschools.org). In Prince George's County, Maryland, Levine is working with high school students to create an "Information Commons" (see www.princegeorges.org). This is an association devoted to building a state-of-the-art web site with asset maps, news articles, structured deliberations, and other public goods.

Meira Levinson is deeply engaged in educational research, policy, and practice. As a researcher, she is currently writing a book on civic and multicultural education in *de facto* segregated schools and communities (Henry Holt, forthcoming in 2006). Her present research is supported by a Bunting Fellowship at the Radcliffe Institute for Advanced Study at Harvard University, a National Academy of Education/Spencer Foundation Post-doctoral Fellowship, a Visiting Scholar position at the Harvard Graduate School of Education, and a grant from the Center for Information and Research on Civic Learning and Engagement (CIRCLE). Levinson's previous publications include *The Demands of Liberal Education* (Oxford University Press, 1999), as well as numerous articles and book chapters. As a practitioner, she is currently in her seventh year of teaching middle school; at present she teaches eighth-grade civics in the Boston Public Schools. Levinson is also engaged in education policy, especially regarding civic education. She was a signatory to the Civic Mission of Schools and serves on the Steering Committee for the Campaign for the Civic Mission of Schools. She also was a member of the American Political Science Standing Committee on Civic Education and Civic Engagement, and she contributed to the Boston Public Schools' development of a district-wide eighth-grade civics curriculum.

Jacob T. Levy is Assistant Professor of Political Science at the University of Chicago, a Mellon Foundation New Directions Fellow at the University of Chicago Law School, and Secretary-Treasurer of the American Society for Political and Legal Philosophy. He has been a National Science Foundation graduate fellow and a Fulbright Scholar, and he has received fellowships from the Social Philosophy and Policy Center and the Earhart Foundation. He is the author of *The Multiculturalism of Fear* (Oxford University Press, 2000) and numerous articles on multiculturalism, nationalism, and indigenous rights. He is currently writing on the historical and contemporary tensions between rationalist and pluralist liberalisms.

Mick (Michael) Womersley is assistant professor of human ecology at Unity College, Maine. He is an experienced social scientist who specializes in community-based case studies applied to environmental problems and a practical policy researcher interested in grassroots investigations. He was once a military airplane mechanic, a rescue party leader for the UK Royal Air Force Mountain Rescue Service, and a leader of backcountry field trips for the University of Montana's Wilderness and Civilization program. His research interests include sustainable development and ecological economics, urban/suburban growth control and planning policy, and sustainable agriculture. Womersley teaches all of these subjects at Unity College, where he lives with his wife Aimee, two dogs, one cat, and eleven rather aged chickens in a home-built, straw bale, solar-powered house.